Scott Berkemeyer

# LAUGHTER IS LEGAL

## BOOKS BY FRANCIS LEO GOLDEN

*Laughter Is Legal*

*Fellow Citizens*

*Jest What the Doctor Ordered*

*For Doctors Only*

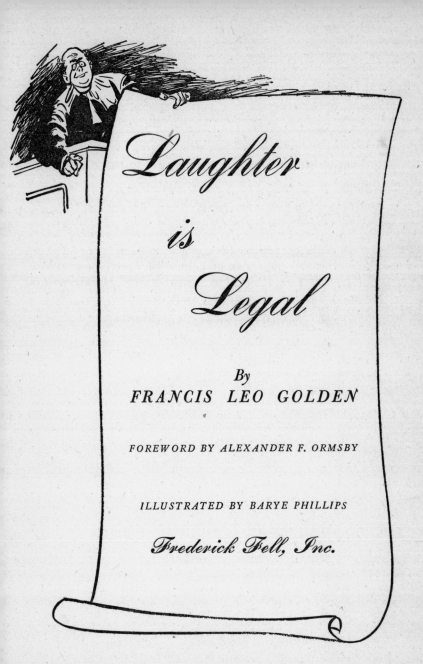

# Laughter
## is
## Legal

By
### FRANCIS LEO GOLDEN

FOREWORD BY ALEXANDER F. ORMSBY

ILLUSTRATED BY BARYE PHILLIPS

Frederick Fell, Inc.

*The author is greatly indebted to a host of friends in the legal profession who have contributed personal reminiscences; to the pungent pages of* CASE AND COMMENT *(Lawyers Cooperative Publishing Company, Rochester, New York); to Sidney Hill, Librarian, New York City Bar Association; to Joseph Lanigan, Assistant Attorney-General, State of New Jersey; and to an army of cartoonists, gag writers, and humorists who live in this great country where* LAUGHTER IS LEGAL.

# Foreword

THE LEGAL PROFESSION has been for years the target of unde-
served calumny. There are standard jokes, cartoons, and gags
that pillory the lawyer to his eternal discomfiture. It might
be well to review them in this foreword so that we may
dispose of them for all time.

Francisco Quevedo, the contemporary of Cervantes, had an
acidic contempt for the lawyers of his era. In a Dante-like
argosy into the nether regions, Quevedo asks his Satanic
Highness, "Why do you place the lawyers in the same corner
of hell as the artillerymen?"

"Because," said Lucifer, "both are eternally waging war on
humanity."

Quevedo had other barbs to sling at us. A lawyer is one
who picks your pocket and shows you a law for it. A lawyer
is like a cartwheel . . . he must be greased before he'll
move. And here, all these years, as dean of a law school, I
have been telling my bright young men and women that the
legal profession forms the strongest fabric of society. That we
knit laws together that men may have a refuge for Justice
and Equity. Then along comes another 18th Century "wit"
who chirps, "Law and Equity are two things God hath
joined together but which man hath put asunder." You see
what I mean?

The lawyer does not produce and sell a physical commod-
ity as do the farmer and the grocer. He does not make den-

tures nor carve gold inlays as the dentist does. His medium
is one of intangibles. He deals in a "service" that is seldom
appreciated and more often misunderstood. Enters ribald
comment. The jokesmith has the burglar leaving our house
and when his companion asks him, "What did you get?"
the first burglar answers, "It's a lawyer's home." Then the
second burglar inquires, "What did you lose?"

———•—•———

Glenn R. Winters, Secretary of the American Judicature
Society, joins me in an attitude of concern that the bench and
bar's notable contributions to humanity may be menaced by
the unfairness of certain legal humor. The jokes and wise-
cracks that point up the failings of one weak professional
brother should not be a measuring stick of the entire membership of a noble profession.

But the gagsters turn out the same drivel yearly. "A client
between two lawyers is like a fish between two cats." Or it
varies to "A lawyer rescues your estate from your enemies
that he may keep it himself." Two lawyers in court castigate
each other. One calls the other an unmitigated liar. The other
retorts, "You're an idiotic scoundrel." Whereupon the judge
says, "Now that the attorneys have identified each other, let's
proceed with the case." And so on, *ad nauseam*.

In ancient days we had the ridicule of Sir John Hamilton.
"An attorney is like a porcupine. It's impossible to touch
him without pricking one's finger." Someone advertised a
farm for sale in that era and, after extolling the virtues of
good soil and salubrious climate, appended this last line, "Not
a lawyer within fifteen miles."

———•—•———

Quite often, as lawyers, we expect such acerbity. Sometimes when we're satirized, it's our own fault. After George

**FOR SALE**

HOUSE, EXCELLENT
CONDITION, NEAR
SCHOOL, GOOD ROADS,
LOW PRICE--NOT A
LAWYER WITHIN
FIFTEEN MILES.

Ade had finished a speech at a banquet, the lawyer-toast-master, thrusting his hands into his pockets as he arose, said, "Doesn't it seem strange that a professional humorist can be funny?"

Ade jumped to his feet and replied, "Doesn't it seem strange to see a lawyer with his hands in his own pockets?"

Even Abraham Lincoln, our own brother member of the bar, let us down when he tarried at the town tavern the evening before a case was to be heard in the local courthouse. When Abe reached the inn, the huge fireplace in the sitting room was surrounded by all the other lawyers interested in the case. "A very cold night," said the innkeeper.

"Colder than hell," replied Abe.

A bystander inquired, "You've been there, too, Mr. Lincoln?"

"Oh, yes," smiled Abe, "and it's just as it is here. All the lawyers are nearest the fire."

So it's readily seen we've been roasted to a crisp by humorists, real and alleged. That's why it's pleasing as well as entertaining to read this book by Francis Leo Golden, who, in his past delineations of medical humor, *For Doctors Only* and *Jest What the Doctor Ordered*, performed a fine service in public relations for the medical profession. This book of legal and political humor has high standards of selectivity. There are stories that reveal some facet of human nature set against the backdrop of the courtroom. There are stories portraying our foibles and quirks of character in the lawyer's office, in the constant conflict with crime and the rapidly changing mores and customs of our progressive era. There are anecdotes and epigrams for judge and jury; for counsel and witness; for all who enjoy sustained and hearty laughter. It is a book that humanizes but never ridicules; it pokes gentle fun without a trace of meanness. It is a book that has long been eagerly awaited by the legal profession.

ALEXANDER F. ORMSBY
*Dean, John Marshall College of Law*
*Jersey City, New Jersey*

# Contents

FOREWORD, *by Alexander F. Ormsby*                                    7

INTRODUCTION                                                          15

1. WHEN I PUT OUT TO SEE                                             19
2. PARTICIPLE CRIMINIS                                               34
3. "ORDER IN THE COURT! HAM ON RYE!"                                 45
4. "THE WHOLE TRUTH—AND NOTHING LIKE THE
   TRUTH"                                                            58
5. "JURIES AND OTHER INJURIES"                                       76
6. THE COMEDY OF EROS                                                86
7. THE TIES THAT BLIND                                               99
8. POLICE TO MEET YOU                                               114
9. PEN PALS                                                         136
10. WHEN COMPENSATION SETS IN                                       152
11. AMBULANCE CHASES LAWYER                                         159
12. TORTS AND RETORTS                                               173
13. YOU GOTTA HAVE WILE POWER                                       184
14. JESTICE OF THE PEACE                                            196
15. DON'T MAKE A WILL—IT'S A DEAD GIVE-AWAY                          208
16. ACTIONS SPEAK LOUDER THAN LAWS                                  219
17. HERE COMES THE BRIBE                                            233
18. DEEP IN THE HEART OF TAXES                                      246
19. DON'T CHANGE BOSSES IN MIDSTREAM                                263
20. SUMMATION                                                       277

# Introduction

BECAUSE laughter is a grand tonic we should have more of it. That was the theme of my two excursions into the realm of medical humor. In this book we scan the courtroom, the legislative halls, and all due process of law, to unearth and reveal the true, enduring humor of law and politics.

What is humor? Is it the sum total of all human experiences exposed by penetrating satire? Is it our bombast and vanity brought before the distorting mirrors of the amusement park? Every time that droll, Frank Sullivan, attempted a definition of humor, he felt stymied. But he thought humor was best enacted by a musical comedy scene wherein Harry Watson, the comedian, had ordered a plate of soup.

The headwaiter was solicitous. "How do you like the soup?"

Harry was glum, morose. "I'm sorry I stirred it," he said.

Humor is the refusal to take yourself, your institutions, your customs, your way of life seriously. Humor punctures evil and looks flippantly at the follies of life. Irvin S. Cobb, who greatly amused an earlier generation of Americans, studied Mark Twain as a model for all humorists. Cobb was convinced that the Twain formula was simply this: "Look what fools we are and I am at the head of the procession."

The profession of law and the art of politics have long been overlooked for their great contributions to *Humor Americana*. We believe Exhibit A would be a Peter Arno cartoon that appeared in the *New Yorker*. The fond mother is telling her friend, "My son has his law degree and a small, furnished office. It's just a question now of getting him out of bed."

Or take the retort of a politician to an aggressive young attorney at a banquet. "Your remarks, Counsellor, are quite appropriate. Where did you appropriate them from?"

*"Your remarks, Counsellor, are quite appropriate. Where did you appropriate them from?"*

In this book there is a parade of judges, jurymen, witnesses, and lawyers. Here you will see that under the laws of this country a man is innocent until he is proved guilty. Then, if he isn't insane, he is pardoned. Here you will become casualty-minded when you discover the law gives pedestrians the right of way but makes no provision for funeral costs. Here you will encounter the sardonic irony of Abraham Lincoln, a great courtroom lawyer in his era. Mr. Lincoln recalled the man who murdered both his parents and then pleaded for mercy on the ground that he was now an orphan. All of which is ample evidence that we're living in an unpredictable country. Our F.B.I. tells us that crime doesn't pay, and the Internal Revenue Bureau, suing our more successful racketeers, proves that it does.

And as for politics! Here you will see the men who repair their fences by hedging. Here you will find the most *promising* of all careers. And you'll meet the mayor who'll give you the key to the city after he has taken everything valuable out of it. But these are mere transitory phases of a great art. You will find the simple, honest souls, such as the candidate who ran on the platform that he was "good to his mother." That meant he held the lamp while she chopped the wood.

This book has no message. It preaches no doctrine. It is written solely for laughter. It twits both lawyer and politician but it harbors no antipathy. We believe . . . and these pages should prove it . . . that every day in every way the lawyer is the integrating influence of our social order, and that our civic leaders and administrative officers are conjoined with the legal profession in that lofty endeavor.

If in the process we pause for laughter, let us, the laity, have these whimsical moments. For it is merely retributive justice. In real life they lock up the witnesses and let the prisoner out on bail.

Francis Leo Golden

# CHAPTER 1

# When I Put Out to See

How MUCH moaning there'll be at the bar when the young lawyer opens his office depends upon many factors. His relatives, for example. Uncle Jake has held up a mortgage foreclosure for six months waiting for a nephew to handle it without fee. Aunt Esmerelda has had a hankering to tie the can to husband Adelbert, but now with her nephew a lawyer here's a chance to obtain a divorce for nothing. If the nephew asks Auntie, "What about the court costs?", Esmerelda floors him with her answer. "Even when Adelbert was courtin' me, he never spent a dime. So how can there be any court costs?"

Then there is cousin Montmorency, an ex-Quiz Kid. He tackles the young lawyer at the family dinner party celebrating the opening of the new law office. "If a man had a peacock and it went into another man's yard and laid an egg, whom would the egg belong to?" Everyone at the table gazes at the new lawyer for the brightest answer ever to issue from his lips. "That's easy, Monty, the egg would belong to the man who owned the peacock. But he could be prosecuted for trespassing if he went on the other man's property to retrieve the egg." Then the ex-Quiz Kid leers, "Huh, a helluva lawyer you'll make. Did you know that a peacock cannot lay an egg?"

By the time dinner has been served, the waiter has whispered in your ear, "Could I evict a tenant within ninety days?" and the aged doorman outside wants to know the operations of the Old Age Survivors Insurance Act. Your first month in business brings you a record number of clients, none of whom has even fifty cents for a retainer. Then into your office steps a smartly-dressed slickeroo who asks, "How would you like to handle some collections for me? Old accounts, you know." You grasp at this business because your own education begins the moment you can collect for the advice and service you have been giving away freely.

———•———

The young lawyer starts his practice knowing practically everything about everything. He ends up knowing nothing about anything due to his frequent association with judges and laymen.

One young lawyer cast longing eyes at a prosperous city in the south and wrote to a classmate, "What are the prospects in your state for a lawyer who is honest and/or Republican?"

His classmate answered, "As a competent lawyer you have a fair chance at success. As a Republican, the game laws will protect you."

Within a year, no matter where you practice, you have acquired legal "savvy." When you are spotted by a discerning friend carrying a load of books into court, he will ask you, "I thought you carried all the law in your head?" Your answer is brief. "I do. These books are for the judge."

———•———

If you decide to serve in another law firm, rather than open your own office, you run into a severe economic problem. John B. McCallum, a lawyer of Atlanta, Georgia, says this poem is anonymous. But it well describes the law firm that advertises for a man who's admitted to practice and can handle diversified work.

He must know the proceedings
Relating to pleadings,
The ways of preparing a brief;
Must argue with unction
For writs of injunction
As well as for legal relief.

He must form corporations
And have consultations,
Assuming a dignified mien;
Should reach each decision
And legal provision
Wherever the same may be seen.

Attachments and trials,
Specific denials,
Demurrers, replies, and complaints,
Disbursements, expenses,
And partial defenses,
Ejectments, replevins, distraints;

Estoppels, restrictions,
Constructive evictions,
Agreements implied and express,
Accountings, partitions,
Estates, and commissions,
Incumbrances, fraud, and duress.

Above are essentials,
The best of credentials
Required—and handsome physique;
Make prompt application—
Will pay compensation
Of seventeen dollars a week.

So for seventeen dollars a week you must (a) be an advocate of human rights before the law; (b) be a proponent of
liberty and champion of order, and (c) redress wrongs, dis-

courage quarrels, promote justice, and encourage mediation.

When you arrive home you are greeted by wifely sneers. "What do you mean, you've been working like a horse?"

So you tell her. "I've been drawing conveyances all day; helping people who are saddled with debt; advising clients to lead a more stable life; and pleading with judges that the murder bullet didn't come from my man's Colt . . . so you'll pardon me if I now go up to the stall shower and then hit the hay."

———— • • ————

As a lawyer you have such problems as competition from laymen. Recently an item in the papers stated that all labor unions and trade groups were making compulsory a study of law by its membership. This is what we envision in a few years.

There's a dismal future looming for the lawyer,
He will not advise humanity much more,
   And many advocates
   Will be forced to lower rates
Or solicit legal work from door to door.

For it seems that our mechanics and their wives
Are spending leisure time on legal tomes,
   And the law of costs and courts
   And of testaments and torts
Are being now discussed in all our homes.

No wonder that our counsellors look anxious
And seek consolement at the other bar,
   There are no more legal giants
   If someone steals our clients—
Yes, the laity can carry things too far.

———— • • ————

The question of legal fees always worries the laity. In St. Louis a lawyer whispered to his client, "It looks good for our side. The judge's charge was in our favor."

"I'm not worried about the judge's charge," answered the client. "I'm concerned over what your charge will be."

———•—•———

A lawyer in Columbus, Ohio, always thought his fees reasonable and was therefore affronted when one of his influential clients offered him a leather wallet as settlement for his fee.

"I hand-tooled this myself," said the client.

The lawyer was gruff and angrily retorted, "I do not believe you understand that my services are to be paid in cash, not gifts."

The client was upset. "How much is your fee?"

"Five hundred dollars," answered the lawyer.

The client reached into the wallet, extracted a thousand dollars in bills, drew off five hundred, and paid the lawyer.

———•—•———

Then there was the lawyer who joined the nudist colony. He never had a suit afterwards.

———•—•———

Foremost in the mind of the lawyer is not the immediate court, but how the case will fare on appeal. It has been explained in doggerel:

> The lawyer fell on a banana skin,
> His torn clothes made him feel
> That, as the legal words explain—
> His suit was lost on a peel.

But Anthony C. Tomczak, of Chicago, quotes Justice Larson of the Supreme Court of Utah (Pennock vs. Newhouse Realty Company) for a more descriptive summary of the suit that's lost on appeal.

"Counsel is not responsible for and has no control over the facts, but the pleadings are his offspring, sired by his knowledge and dammed by his ingenuity, and they should be his pride and joy. It is far better that such offspring die aborning than to live until charged with the duty of supporting a judgment, and then die an ignominious death upon the gallows of the Appellate Court."

In the Supreme Court of Mississippi with Chief Justice Whitfield presiding, there was a taxation matter, the Yazoo and Mississippi Valley Railroad vs. the State.

Former Judge Beckett represented the State. He had lost the case in the circuit court and had appealed to the Supreme Court of Mississippi.

On the day of trial Beckett placed thirty large law volumes on the desk and began to read excerpts from each one.

Justice Whitfield, always exasperated at lawyers who read from books, spoke, "The court thinks that counsel might assume that the court knows some law."

Beckett's reply was, "Yes, that's what I assumed in the court below, and that's the reason I represent appellants here today."

———•—•———

Robert Ingersoll summed up the subject of fees, legal and otherwise.

"How can we ever show our appreciation?" a woman asked him, after one of his brilliant lectures.

"My dear lady," replied Ingersoll, "ever since the Phoenicians invented money, there has been only one answer to that question."

The same question disturbed counsellor Maurice A. Ross when he stepped before District Court Judge Philip Vine in Trenton. "Your honor, my client has a replevin suit against him, involving only a few hundred dollars. I am not prepared to go on with the case today and I respectfully ask for a two-week adjournment."

"Why?" asked the judge.

"My client is in Pennsylvania training for a prizefight."

"I'm not interested in such a reason."

"Candidly, your honor, I am. He's fighting for my fee."

———•—•———

Maurice Rose was in the same mood as a young lawyer in Duluth, who said to his associate, "I feel like telling that judge where to get off again."

"What do you mean—again?"

"I felt like it last week."

———•—•———

We hope Jack Goodman and Fred Schwed, Jr., won't mind a slight switch in one of their stories, inasmuch as we stick to the essential "meat."

The young wife of a Hollywood lawyer is a friend of Elizabeth Taylor. So when Miss Taylor had some tax problem, her friend brought her to the husband's office. Later the lawyer said to his new office boy, "Know who that was my wife brought in?"

"No, sir. Who?"

"That, son, was Elizabeth Taylor!"

"Gee, Mr. Burlap! Which one was Taylor?"

The lawyer gazed pensively at his office boy. "Here, Gerald," he said. "Here is a dollar you've just earned. Not that I think you are going to need it. But I would appreciate your throwing a little business my way in a year or two, after you've become rich and famous."

———•—•———

The *New Yorker,* some years ago, related an incident in the education of a young legalite.

A young lawyer got his first client and had to appear on his behalf at city court. A fledgling attorney's first court appearance is a big occasion for him, and this fellow waited with bridelike excitement for his case to be called. When the word finally came, he laid his hat and coat on a bench and stepped before the judge. "Young man, I assume that

this is your first experience in this court," the judge said
sternly.

With that awful what-have-I-done? feeling, the lawyer
said, "Yes, sir."

"I thought so," the judge said, fretfully. "Before we proceed, get your hat and coat and put them where you can
watch them."

———— • • ————

The young lawyer might well consider a problem presented by Mr. Winslow.

Joe Smith applies to Mr. White to become a law clerk,
offering to pay him the customary fee as soon as he shall
have won his first suit in law. To this Mr. White formally
agrees and admits young Smith to the privileges of the office.
But the time without his fees drags out so long that Lawyer
White tires of waiting and determines to sue his pupil for
the amount.

He reasons in this manner: If I win this case, Smith will
be compelled to pay me by the decision of the court; if I
lose it, he will have to pay me by the condition of our contract, for he will have won his first lawsuit.

But Smith is not alarmed when he learns his teacher's
intention because of his reasoning, which is:

If I succeed, and the award of the court is in my favor, of
course I shall not have to pay the money; if the court decides
against me, I shall not have to pay it, according to the terms
of our contract, as I shall not yet have gained my first suit
in law.

———— • • ————

Eddie Jaffe passes this along.

Noticing a piece of paper fluttering under the windshield
wiper of a new car parked in the street, a curious New
Yorker stopped to read it. On the paper was neatly written:
"Attorney—am inside attending to business."

Below, also neatly written, was this: "Policeman—I attended to mine outside." And on the door was a parking ticket.

———•———

In his advice to a young lawyer, Justice Joseph Story once wrote:

> "Be brief, be pointed, let your matter stand
>   Lucid in order! Solid and at hand;
> Spend not your words on trifles, but condense,
>   Strike with the mass of thought, not drops of sense."

In the time of the Roman Empire, a client would have appreciated such advice if it had been taken by his lawyer. As related by Martial, the client had a justifiable squawk. He said to his lawyer, "O, Sir Advocate, my case has nothing to do with violence, murder, or poison. I merely accuse my neighbor of having stolen my three goats. You, however, with all the strength of your voice and with a pounding upon the table with your fist, shout only about the Battle of Cannae, the war of Mithridates, the perfidy of the Carthaginians, and about Sulla, Marius, and Mucius. Say something, I beseech you, about my three goats."

———•———

Cordell Hull is an extremely cautious speaker, striving always for scientific accuracy. One day on a train, a friend pointed to a fine flock of sheep grazing in a field. "Look. Those sheep have just been sheared," he said.

Hull studied the flock. "Sheared on this side, anyway," he admitted.

———•———

Equally cautious was the reply of Abraham Lincoln, while practicing law at Springfield, Illinois, to a New York firm inquiring as to the financial standing of a fellow townsman: "First of all, he has a wife and a baby; together they ought

to be worth $500,000 to any man. Secondly, he has an office
in which there is a table worth $1.50, and three chairs worth,
say, $1. Last of all, there is in one corner a large rathole,
which will bear looking into. Respectfully, A. Lincoln."

———•—•———

Speaking of Lincoln, a lawyer in Wilmington halted his
son on the way to a night of frivolity. "Son, when Abe Lincoln was your age, he was busily studying law every night."

The son yawned. "Yeah, and when he was your age, Dad,
he was President."

———•—•———

The lawyer's wife confided to her maid, "I think my husband is having an affair with his stenographer."

The maid was appalled. "I don't believe it. You're only
saying that to get me jealous."

———•—•———

He might have been the lawyer who advertised in the
local paper:

> HELP WANTED: BUSY LAWYER SEEKS ALERT
> YOUNG WOMAN TO ACT AS DECEPTIONIST.

———•—•———

A thrifty man went to a lawyer for advice. After the inter-
view the man met an acquaintance and told him about it.

"But why spend money on a lawyer?" asked the other.
"When you sat in his office, did you see all the law books
there? Well, what he told you, you could read in those law
books."

"You're right," admitted the advice seeker, "but that
lawyer—he knows what page it's on."

———•—•———

The young lawyer brought his problem to the old lawyer.

"Son," said the old man, "I was just playing my favorite
composition, *Traumerei,* when you walked in."

"Why do you tell me this?"

"Because Robert Schumann always advised would-be composers that in order to compose, it was enough simply to remember a tune which nobody else thought of. Evasive? Perhaps. But I would tell you this, my boy, a good lawyer will remember every case that every judge has forgotten."

———•—•———

The ardent advocacy of the client's case is the lawyer's solemn obligation. A rural lawyer in England upheld this principle staunchly before Chief Justice Cockburn.

The Chief Justice was becoming irritable over the valuable hours consumed in the trial. He reprimanded the country lawyer. "Mr. Jones, time is passing."

Mr. Jones responded. "Let it pass, my lord."

"But there are other cases to be heard."

"Yes, my lord, but this is the only one my client is interested in."

———•—•———

Apocryphal or not, the late Max Steuer was said to have billed a client for $500 for answering a simple legal question while both were washing up in the men's room.

Two weeks later they met again in the same place. "It's raining outside, Max," said the other. "And, remember, I'm telling you, not asking."

———•—•———

A prominent lawyer in Newark met a Common Pleas judge at the annual Bar dinner. It was a convivial night and both of them had imbibed heavily.

The following morning the lawyer had a case before the judge. But he had a head-pounding hangover and he knew in his muddled mind he couldn't do justice to his client. He advanced to the bench.

"Your honor, I would like a postponement of this case."

"On what grounds?"

"Wet grounds," said the lawyer.

"Granted," said the judge, with a friendly wink.

———•—•———

There's a humorous philosophy of the law expounded by William M. Blatt, of Boston, that rates being cited here:

There are only two kinds of women clients—those who pay liberally and those who complain to the Bar Association.

The average man thinks lawyers are dishonest because if he were a lawyer he would be dishonest.

He who would travel from law to logic must jump many fences.

———•—•———

There was still one fence to be jumped by a litigant who had to leave on a long journey before the conclusion of a lawsuit he had brought against a neighbor. He left instructions with his lawyer that the verdict should be sent to him by telegraph.

Two days later he received this telegram: "Right has triumphed."

At once he wired back: "Appeal immediately."

———•—•———

A salesman had sold everything that was necessary for the furnishing of the lawyer's office, when he had a happy thought.

"Oh, yes, I nearly forgot," he exclaimed, "you need a doormat!"

"Fine! But bring me one that is well worn."

———•—•———

As the Elliots point out in their excellent book, *The Work of the Advocate*: "The first step cannot safely be taken in a case without a settled and certain theory. A case must be put to trial upon a definite theory. That theory—the pleadings must outline . . . the evidence sustain . . . and the law support."

But suppose, after such procedure, you do not encounter, "the cold neutrality of an impartial judge," as Edmund Burke phrased it.

As a young barrister, the Earl of Birkenhead protested a judge's obvious sympathy for his opponent's side. The judge rebuked him and their remarks developed a distinctly personal flavor. Finally the exasperated judge exclaimed, "Young man, you are extremely offensive."

"As a matter of fact," said the earl, "we both are. But I am trying to be, and you can't help it."

---

The briefcase a certain lawyer carried belied the length of his every argument. He was so verbose, such a long-winded bore, that one judge said to him, "If I knew you were coming, I'd have faked an ache."

Once he addressed the judge, "Am I trespassing on the court's time?"

"Young man," said the judge, "you are not making that fine distinction between trespassing on the court's time and encroaching on eternity."

In one case this lawyer had looked up precedents dating back to Julius Caesar. Two hours later, while he was still gassing away, he noticed the court was inattentive.

"Begging your honor's pardon," said he, "but do you follow me?"

The judge shifted uneasily in his chair. "I have so far," he answered, "but I'll say frankly that, if I thought I could find my way back, I'd quit right here."

---

One of the justices of the Supreme Court tells of another young lawyer in the west who was trying his first case before Justice Harlan. The youthful attorney had evidently conned his argument until he knew it by heart.

Before he had consumed ten minutes in his oratorical

effort, the justice had decided the case in his favor and told him so. Despite this, the young lawyer would not cease. He had attained such a momentum that he could not stop.

Finally, Justice Harlan leaned forward and, in the politest of tones, said: "Mr. Smith, despite your arguments, the court has concluded this case in your favor."

In Johnson vs. Emerson, an English law case in 1871, Baron Bramwell said, "A client is entitled to say to his counsel—'I want your advocacy, not your judgment. I prefer that of the court.'"

A vigorous oratorical counsel, after stating the facts, began an emotional appeal to the jury—"And now, gentlemen, I will drop the advocate and assume the *man*."

"Oh, no," interrupted the judge, "it is only as an advocate that you are entitled to address the jury—as a *man* you have no right to trouble them."

Maybe there is this fine distinction between the advocate and the man. At least it puzzled the vapid, buxom blonde in a Richter cartoon.

She is being led down the courthouse steps by her elderly lawyer, who has a possessive clutch on her arm and that certain look in his eye.

The dumb but beautifully-shaped dame looks up at the lawyer and asks, "Just what did the judge mean, Mr. Bowen, when he said he was releasing me in your custody?"

According to Francis L. Wellman, an English judge, when asked what is necessary to win a court case, replied:

"First you need a good case, then you need good evidence, then you need good witnesses, then you need a good jury, and then you need good luck."

Counsellor Bert Lefkowitz had none of these. His client didn't help, either. When the judge was ready for sentence, he asked Bert's client, "Have you anything to offer the court before sentence is passed?"

"No, Judge," he answered, "I couldn't even give you a buck. The expenses of this trial have taken my last dollar."

———•———

Name all the quandaries of the youthful lawyer and you cannot equal that uncertain moment when inexperience halts his flow of thought.

He was dictating to his stenographer and he was in doubt on the phraseology. He looked at her and asked, "Do you retire a loan?"

Her eyes flashed. "I'll have you know I sleep with Mama.'

# CHAPTER 2

# Participle Criminis

"Just what did your medical report show, Doctor?" asked the defendant's counsel.

"I examined the tissue under the microscope and detected squamos epithelium with normal margins. The central portion was markedly thickened and keratonization had increased. These papillary-like projections in some areas showed distinct calcification. The underlying fibrous connective-tissue stroma revealed no pathology."

"In simple, everyday language, Doctor, what did the plaintiff have?"

The doctor looked sheepishly at the judge, and answered, "A wart."

———•———

In another court action in Milwaukee, an engineer, arrested for a traffic accident, was testifying. "Circumstances got beyond my control. The wheels accelerated in one plane while the force of gravity operated in an angle to the rotating plane. This produced a rotation perpendicular to the plane of the wheel rotation."

The judge pondered this one for several minutes. "What does all this flummery mean?"

The engineer answered: "My car skidded."

———•———

Every day in our courtrooms we are mystified, badgered, provoked, and perplexed by the peculiarities of the language.

Legal English has become so obsolete that we wonder why our judicial systems tolerate its continued usage. Too frequently is the law circumvented by legal verbiage whose origins are tied up with ancient mumbo-jumbo and dead customs.

It isn't the lawyer's fault that he must vindicate the law as it is handed down to him. He must buttress and fortify his case by arguments, evidence, and forms that are woefully outmoded. He must perpetuate legal abracadabra and ancient phraseology no matter how it bedazzles and befuddles his client. What we need to strip excess verbiage from the *Corpus Juris* is the Malaproprian directness of a Sam Goldwyn when he said, "A verbal contract isn't worth the paper it's printed on." At least, we know what Sam means.

———•—•———

The law has couched itself in solemn, mystical, and equivocal sentences which can be interpreted by any judge in any way he wishes. Let's abolish cobweb subtleties, no matter how finely spun, that justice will always triumph. Justice Oliver Wendell Holmes' opinions were enduring examples of lucidity and brevity. You know what the language means when you read it.

Recently over the radio we heard the intricacies of legal terms given another beating. The dulcet-toned quizmaster asked, "What does it mean to die intestate?"

The housewife pondered the verbal pitfall before she squeaked her answer, "It's when you die of intestinal trouble."

———•—•———

In Utica a witness was asked, "Do you know whether the milk from this dairy is pasteurized?"

"It sure is," was the answer. "Every morning they turn their cows out to pasture."

The character of Mrs. Malaprop in Sheridan's *The Rivals* has endured these many years in our courtrooms, adding another problem to legal life.

There was the divorce-seeking woman who told the judge, "I want my freedom and I also crave ammonia."

"Ammonia? You mean alimony. Sweet spirits of ammonia is used to wake people up."

"Getting money outa *him,* Judge, will wake him up."

———•———

And in Davenport, Iowa, on cross-examination, a lawyer asked a witness, "If you're evicted from your home, do you have any tentative plans?"

"No," answered the man, "I never could sleep in one of those tents."

———•———

Someone had wired a government bureau asking whether hydrochloric acid could be used to clean a given type of boiler tube. The answer was: "Uncertainties of reactive processes make use of hydrochloric acid undesirable where alkalinity is involved."

The inquirer wrote back, thanking the bureau for the advice, saying that he would use hydrochloric acid. The bureau wired him: "Regrettable decision involves uncertainties. Hydrochloric will produce submuriate invalidating reactions."

Again the man wrote thanking them for their advice, saying that he was glad to know that hydrochloric acid was all right. This time the bureau wired in plain English:

"Hydrochloric acid," said the telegram, "will eat hell out of your tube."

———•———

The law clerk stuck his head into the office of the senior member of the firm. "Mr. Wintersled just called. He cannot be in court today. He fell down and sprained a liniment."

Counsellor Eddie DeSevo leaned over the table and spoke to his client. "When I address the judge and jury, I'll plead for clemency."

The client wasn't at all pleased. "Why don't you just plead for me and let Clemency get his own lawyer?"

———— • • ————

No Malapropist could equal a detective in the Jersey City Police Department.

One night at a banquet Congressman Ed Hart asked the detective how he had enjoyed the food.

"Congressman," said Officer Malaprop, "I've never before tasted filet mongols like these."

This detective liked coffee "cooked in them new-fangled fertilizers," and he once bought an automobile with huge shock "observers" on them.

When asked if the modern patrolman excelled the officer of other years, the detective said, "Sure he does. Today he has better medication."

The one truthful Malapropism he came up with was on March 15th. He addressed his income tax return to the Bureau of Eternal Revenue.

———— • • ————

George E. Cutley asked his client the direct question. "Before I take your case, I want the truth. Did you commit this crime?"

"No, George," he replied, "I didn't do it and I can prove a lullaby."

"You mean an alibi."

"No. My wife will testify that at that hour I was singing the baby to sleep."

———— • • ————

When Molly Perlman was injured while getting off the moving stairway in a New York department store, she sued the store for damages.

When the case came up for trial, Molly was terribly nervous. In her broken English she tried to tell just what had happened, but she had particular difficulty in describing the "thing that runs all the time."

"Escalator," the judge corrected her several times. The woman's confusion increased.

"Chudge," she cried, "pliz dun't esk me later, esk me now."

————•————

Counsellor Lou Gerber, of Princeton, was trying a case in a Mercer County court. The defendant was charged with a statutory violation and he produced a character witness.

The character witness was asked, "What do you know about the chastity of the defendant?"

"Chass-ity? He ain't got no automobile."

————•————

Which reminded Assistant Prosecutor Art Lane of an answer he overheard.

The judge was listening to the testimony and interjected a remark. "Do you claim that this man hit you with malice aforethought?" he asked.

"Judge, you're confusing me. I said he hit me with a Ford, and I stick to it."

————•————

The state's attorney in Chicago was once questioning a Capone mobster. "Do you have any partners in chicanery?"

"Naw," muttered the reluctant witness, "but I once had a partner in Cicero."

————•————

Ernie Glickman hired a new law stenographer. Returning to the office after a consultation in New York, Ernie was anxious about the fate of a client. He had left instructions with the new stenographer to keep in touch with the courthouse.

"What's the news?" he asked the girl. "Has the grand jury returned an indictment?"

She stared at her boss. "Whom did they borrow it from?"

---

Jessica Libby Rakowitz adds an item to this collection.

A clergyman had been on the stand for some time and been subjected to a trying ordeal. After fifteen minutes of cross-examination by opposing counsel, on a small and irrelevant point, the lawyer for the other side was heard to object in the following language.

"The questions are immaterial, incompetent, and *irreverend*." The objection was promptly sustained.

---

Charlie Malloy represented a client in Hunterdon County, New Jersey, who was charged with speeding.

The rural policeman testified that he used three methods to check the rate of speed. "I have a speedometer on my motorcycle, I have a stop-watch, and also a watch on my wrist."

Counsellor Malloy asked a simple question. "Were your chronometers synchronized?"

The policeman answered angrily, "I want you to know, lawyer, that I'm in the best of health."

---

And we must always find a niche in the Malaprop Hall of Fame for the yegg who told his pal, "They held me in jail twenty-four hours on superstition."

---

Another witness who annoyed his cross-examiner was the passive little man who gave a detailed account of his sufferings. "So," asked the lawyer, "you attribute all your subsequent troubles to this automobile accident?"

"I do."

"Yet you seem calm, restrained, patient."

"Yes, I'm like Job," spouted the witness. "I'm in the hands of an all-wise and unscrupulous Providence."

---

The defense counsel pressed the witness for a coherent answer. "Was he a tall man?"

"Nah, he wasn't tall."

"Was he a short man?"

"Nah."

"Well, what was he?"

"I'd say he was mediocre."

---

Perle Mesta, our Minister to Luxembourg, is the darling of Capitol newsmen because of her occasional Malapropisms.

Hearing that a Republican charmer had been appointed to UNESCO by the State Department, Perle exclaimed airily: "Oh, I know all about that organization. I attended a meeting of ESCROW in Paris last fall."

But Perle's deviations of diction can't equal the club-woman in Beacon, New York, who was quoting George Bernard Shaw's statement, "Woman reduces us all to a common denominator."

The clubwoman was challenging Shaw's viewpoint, but her version brought chuckles to the audience. "Woman reduces us all to a common detonator," she said.

Bob Stone, reporting the incident, came up with the classic headline. "This touched off a bombshell."

---

No lawyer ever delighted a courtroom more than Paul Supinski of Jersey City. Paul, of noble Polish birth, was always troubled by the nuances of English, its peculiar idioms and variations.

In Judge Charles Egan's court one day Paul asked a witness, "Where were you when you weren't where you said you were?"

Judge Egan rapped his gavel. "Just a moment. Let me ponder that one, too. Where were you . . . when you weren't where . . . you said you were? Counsellor, I don't think I could answer such a question. Please reframe it."

There was another day when Paul said to a witness, "I show you a piece of coal and I ask you, what is it?"

The witness replied, "A piece of coal."

Paul thanked him. "Yes, that's right."

———•—•———

An applicant for citizenship wasn't too clear about the judge's question, "Do you solemnly swear to support the Constitution?"

He said, "Judge, I'd like to, but I have a wife and six children in Europe."

———•—•———

Let it not be thought from the above examples that desecration of the language characterizes our courts. Far from it.

There has been great rhetoric emanating from bench and bar. Cicero, Bolingbroke, the younger Pitt, Rufus Choate, and Daniel Webster come to mind. Every young attorney should read Cicero's *De Oratore*. And if he has time, Quintilian's *The Education of an Orator,* Aristotle's *Rhetoric,* and Plato's *Phaedrus.*

He will then have the erudition of the young lawyer in the Bronx who was corrected by the judge. "You mean, Counsellor, that the witness in his business affairs is not doing badly."

"What did I say, Judge?"

"Bad."

"But there is a difference, your honor, in the l-y."

"What do you mean?"

"For example," retorted the counsellor, "take a look at the shapely witness. It sure makes a difference if you look at her sternly . . . or at her stern."

Besides rhetoric and syntax, there is also the matter of punctuation. In law, it's very important. We might make a statement, for instance: Woman is pretty, generally speaking.

Now take away the comma and see the difference.

Abe Lewis knew how important this subject was. He said to a new stenographer in his law office, "I hope you understand the importance of punctuation."

"Oh, my, yes," she assured him. "I always get to work on time."

Herbert F. Moore received excellent advice from his lawyer uncle, William A. Moore, when he opened his own law office. "Herb, you'll have a great temptation when you employ a legal stenographer. But always hire the girl on the basis of her grammar, not glamor."

———•—•———

Yes, language can be confusing.

The patrolman was an obtuse, one-track-minded chap. He testified that when he arrested the defendant, he, the defendant, said he was drunk.

Here is the verbatim testimony.

JUDGE: I want his exact words. Just as the prisoner uttered them. He didn't use the pronoun . . . he? Did he?

PATROLMAN: Oh, yes . . . he said *he* was drunk.

JUDGE (impatiently): No, you don't understand. I want the very words he spoke. Did he say: "I was drunk"?

PATROLMAN: You may have been drunk, Judge, but the prisoner didn't mention your name.

PROSECUTOR: Look, Officer, you still don't understand. The judge means . . . did the prisoner say to you: "I was drunk"?

PATROLMAN: He might have said you were drunk, but I didn't hear him mention your name, either.

DEFENSE COUNSEL: Here, let me try. Listen, Officer, in our

English syntax, our English grammar, we have three persons —the first person is I; the second person is you; the third person is he, she, or it. Now . . . did my client, in his exact words, use the first person? Did he say: "I was drunk"?

PATROLMAN: No, Counsellor, he didn't say you was drunk. He said he was drunk, and if you don't stop asking me all these questions, I'm going out and get drunk, too.

---

Another admonition from the older to the younger lawyer concerns the avoidance of pedantic language.

The Harvard mother said, "My son's letters always send me to the dictionary." The Georgetown mother said, "My son's letters always send me to the bank."

There is a difference in the way language is employed. An old country philosopher in Maine said one day, after listening to a professor who used nothing but multi-syllables, "He uses them big words 'cause he's a-feared that if we folks knowed what he was talkin' about, we'd know he don't know what he's talkin' about."

---

The bench can be guilty, too. "You do not have a lawyer?" asked the court.

"No," replied the prisoner.

"Then," said the judge, "I'll appoint one to defend you."

"Please," said the prisoner, "if it's all the same to you, Judge, just give me an interpreter to tell me what you're talking about."

---

Neora E. Fletcher of Grand Junction, Colorado, describes legal language "through a stenographer's eyes."

> Says the layman to the milkman,      19
> "Lemme have some cream."
> Would a lawyer use such language?
> Oh, no, he wouldn't dream

Of making it so easy
For the man to comprehend;
In asking for some cream or milk,
He would words and time expend.

"At your earliest convenience,"
The man of law would say,
Thereby meaning and intending
It be done without delay,
"A little lacteal fluid,
I need today, I find;
Will you please obtain the same for me,
If your cows are so inclined?"

If you know the English language thoroughly, it will help you in every way. Milford P. Johnson illustrates this point.

During a Shriners' convention in Los Angeles one of the downtown boulevards was roped off for a parade. Only official cars with large signs such as POTENTATE and PAST POTENTATE were allowed there; all other traffic was halted or rerouted.

But one ingenious Californian got by the police blockade and drove nonchalantly down the street. His placard read: PAST PARTICIPLE.

# CHAPTER 3

# "Order in the Court!
# Ham on Rye!"

IN ONE of Dorothy Parker's inimitable sketches of Prohibition days, there is a scene at one of the tables in a speakeasy. The girl beams glassy-eyed at her male companion. "Of course, I know it's you, Judge. I'd know your knees anywhere."

Lest anyone in the audience derive the wrong impression about the judge's presence in such a liquefied lamasery, be it noted that one of the functions of the good judge is that he be a kindly man with an understanding heart. Not all of life is revealed at the bench. The good judge must sometimes seek it at the bar.

The judge, says Jurist William H. Grimball, of Charleston, South Carolina, must:

Be a patient soul.

Have the delicate balance of a tight-rope artist.

Know some law. Not too little, not too much.

For no one knows what the law may be from Friday to Monday or until the advance sheets of the West Publishing Company arrive in the office.

Today both judges and lawyers are more formal, conventional, and rigid than they were in the old, circuit-riding

45

era. Then you found the judge a "folksy" sort of fellow who added spice and homespun sagacity to his decisions. It was, too, justice tempered with merry and sustained laughter. The judge of those days, like the jurist mentioned by Secretary of State Acheson, "was often in error, but never in doubt."

We need no other prototype of the kindly, understanding jurist than Judge Semler.

"I had a strange case before me today," remarked Judge Semler, at the dinner table.

"Before you tell me about it," barked Mrs. Semler, "suppose you place your napkin across your knees. Land sakes alive, how many times must I tell you not to stuff your napkin in your collar?"

Judge Semler removed the napkin from his throat.

"Now go on with the story," ordered Mrs. Semler.

"It was most unusual," said the judge. "A strong, able-bodied man of . . . I should say . . . forty years, charged with striking his aged mother. And yet he didn't seem a cruel type. The doctors at the hospital said he was most tender . . . he whimpered and all that. I said to the man, 'I'm ashamed of you, a big, hulking brute hitting your dear old mother. Have you anything to say before I pass sentence?'

"The man looked up at me," continued Judge Semler, "and I noted his woebegone expression. He spoke quite softly, too. 'I have only this to say, your honor. For the past thirty-five years . . . ever since my father died . . . it has been my duty to go down into the cellar every morning and make the fire for Mom. And every one of those mornings, for thirty-five years, my mother would come behind me and show me how the paper should be placed and how to lay the wood . . . and where to apply the match . . . and how soon the coal should be shoveled in. Every morning for thirty-five years. I stood it as long as I could . . . and then I . . . lost my head. I struck her.'

" 'Sentence suspended,' I said to the man," continued Judge Semler, as he sipped his tea. "I can well understand the provocative circumstances."

The judge's hand, absent-mindedly, went to the napkin on his knee. He raised it to his collar and tucked it in. Mrs. Semler sniffed and said nothing.

———•◆•———

Another judge of equal gentleness asked the contrite and penitent prisoner before him, "Have you ever been sent to prison?"

The man's tears plunged down his cheek. "No, your honor."

"There, there, don't cry," said the judge, compassionately, "you're going to be now."

———•◆•———

We could not mention Burlington County without recalling the embarrassment that came to Judge Riggs of the Common Pleas bench. Genial Howard Eastwood, now himself a justice in New Jersey's courts, was then the Prosecutor of the Pleas.

One afternoon, Prosecutor Eastwood was excoriating the defendant, who had deserted his wife and children to set up a love nest with one of the local strumpets. "This man, your honor, would not be in the fix he is if it weren't for his immoral attitude. He has one wife and is now living with another woman. You and I, Judge Riggs, *know how much it costs to keep two women.*"

———•◆•———

When Senator Bob Taft's dad was a Federal Circuit judge in Ohio, he entered a barber's chair and was greeted by the tonsorialist with "Aren't you Judge Taft?" as he began the lathering of the ample jowls.

"Yes, I am," replied the jurist.

"Recall a fellow named Stebbins? You sent him up for twenty years." Taft studied the barber as he carefully stropped the razor. He was a heavy-shouldered individual with a face scarred by contact with a knife. Could this be the fellow Judge Taft had sentenced?

"I do remember," said Taft, weakly. "He was a bad boy."

"He's my brother," said the barber icily. He placed his sharpened razor on the judicial neck. Judge Taft conjured up fanciful pictures with himself the victim of a brother's vengeance. He closed his eyes and mumbled a short prayer.

"You acted properly, Judge," said the barber. "My brother was a thorough rascal. Should be in jail."

Judge Taft relaxed.

———— • • ————

One day in the life of any judge is eventful. Take these exhibits.

"Your father," thundered the judge, "was a thief and now you're here before me charged with the same crime."

"Can I help it, Judge, if I follow in my father's finger-prints?"

During the hearing of a case, the judge was disturbed by a youth who kept moving about in the rear of the court.

"Young man," exclaimed the judge, "you are making a good deal of unnecessary noise. What are you doing?"

"I have lost my overcoat and am trying to find it," replied the offender.

"Well," said the judge, "people often lose whole suits in here without all that fuss."

It was a warm day, and a dull case concerning the rights of certain river commissioners was being argued in court. Counsel made speeches of interminable length, and the judge fell into a doze.

"But we must have water, your honor," thundered the

defending lawyer in such stentorian tones that the judge awakened.

"All right," he mumbled hastily, "but only a very little in mine."

———— •◆• ————

A judge in Brooklyn, named Dunn, sat patiently listening to a moronic type of witness who repeatedly answered every question with a cryptic, "Who, me?"

For example, the attorney cross-examining her would say, "And were you, on this morning of September 18th, crossing Montague Street around noontime?"

The witness chirped, "Who, me?"

"Yes, you, madam, and did you speak to Officer O'Reilly at that time?"

"Who, me?"

"Yes, you." Turning to the bench the attorney pleaded, "Please, your honor, would you instruct the witness that these questions are directly aimed at her answers?"

"You are the witness, madam," said kindly Justice Dunn, "and you will refrain from such answers as 'Who, me?' Proceed, Counsellor."

The witness began to cry. "I'm just a poor woman not used to this place. I'm trying to do my best. I'm here to see justice done."

Whereupon the judge raised his head and asked, "Who, me?"

———— •◆• ————

Until 1887 New Jersey's high courts had a law judge and two lay judges. That year the lay judges were abolished. But in Burlington County the local Bar Association, to mark their devotion to one lay judge who had served for forty-one years, tendered the old fellow a dinner.

When he responded to their laudations, he said, "It has been a memorable forty-one years. I would not exchange one day of it for all the wealth of the world. I've seen many of you, now grown gray in the law, enter my courtroom as fledglings. Today you are honored members of a great profession. Your toastmaster asked me a few minutes ago if my relations all during these years with my associates on the bench were harmonious. Well, candidly, I can tell you that the only time in forty-one years that the law judge ever consulted me was three weeks ago when he leaned over and said, 'Doesn't your ass ever get tired from sitting on these hard boards?'"

———•—•———

County Judge Richard P. Robbins had an elderly colored grandmother approach him on the bench one morning. "Jedge," she said, "I gotta get me a marr'ge license for my granddaughter. The man in the city clerk's office tol' me to call on you. It's a matter of age."

"How old is your granddaughter?"

"Fifteen."

"She's too young for marriage, madam, according to our laws."

The old lady was tearful. "What I'm gonna do? She's old enuf, Jedge, to do what she's already did."

———•—•———

A famous judge came late to court
    One day in busy season,
Whereat his clerk, in great surprise,
    Inquired, "What's the reason?"
"A child was born," his honor said,
    "And I'm the happy sire."
"An infant judge?" "Oh, no," he said,
    "As yet, he's but a crier."

———•—•———

The difficult part of any judge's day is the ruling out of hearsay evidence. Most witnesses do not understand that they can speak only on what they saw. One judge in Detroit found the solution.

"Hearsay testimony," he explains, "is merely having a fine sense of rumor."

———— • ————

Joe Culloo, confidential aide to Judge James Coolahan, of Hudson County, New Jersey, was approached one night by a whispering friend. "I've got to see the judge tonight. Where can I see him?"

"I'm sorry," said Culloo, "but he is having dinner with his wife and I know he hates to be disturbed after court hours."

"But I must see him," insisted the other.

Culloo smiled. "I told you it's impossible."

"Why?"

"Well, if you must know," retorted Culloo, "his honor is at steak."

———— • ————

Since one story reminds the raconteur of another, we recall some years ago when a Tammany Hall chieftain accosted the late Bill Griffin, publisher of the New York *Enquirer*.

"Bill, did I hear you say there was to be a banquet tendered Judge John O'Brien?"

"No," said Griffin. "I merely remarked that I saw John dining in Manny Wolfe's restaurant and there was a big dinner in his honor this evening."

———— • ————

Life is not all a bed of roses for the judge. We hereby rise to his defense. If he lives in a state where he is chosen by the governor with the advice and consent of the senate, he has just as many stumbling blocks to another term on the bench as though he were living in a state where judges are elected by the people. If his state senator is against him, the path to appointment is temporarily blocked. There must be quiet meetings and some attempt at compromise.

It is axiomatic that a governor should "consult" with the senate on most of his appointments. Such a huddle allows the brimstone and sulphur to waft skyward until the air clears in the perfect aura of understanding.

Out from the conference with the governor nimbly steps the state senator to tell waiting newsmen that "everything was settled amicably. When I said three weeks ago that Judge Knitfuzz could not tell a tort from a tart, I was merely fooling. I have just discovered that the judge's decision, entitled 'Knitfuzz on Knuckleworst,' has been singled out by *Law Reports* as the outstanding decision in this celebrated issue. I am happy to go along with the governor on the appointment."

And for all that Judge Knitfuzz goes through, he runs into days of abuse and misunderstanding. Mark the exhibits, please:

(1) "What makes you say so emphatically," asks the judge, "that these turkeys were stolen from you?"

"I know my turkeys," insists the witness.

"But I have a turkey farm, too," adds the judge, "and I have birds like these in my yard."

"So what?" bristles up the witness. "These turkeys here in the courtroom for evidence are not the only ones that have been stolen from me."

(2) The case is one where a young lady had called another unprintable names. The D.A. puts the plaintiff on the stand. "Tell us what the accused said."

"I just can't," pleads the witness. "It's not for any decent ears to hear."

"Well, then," says the D.A., "suppose you whisper it to his honor."

(3) The prisoner has no lawyer to defend him.

"You want me to appoint a lawyer?" asks the judge.

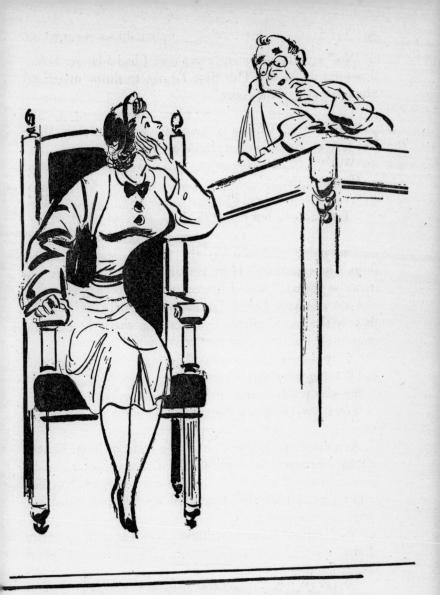

*"If your testimony isn't fit for decent ears, suppose you whisper it to his honor."*

"No," says the prisoner, "every time I had a lawyer before I wound up in jail. This time I'd like to throw myself on the ignorance of the court."

———————

The witness, who was Swedish, was testifying about the size of the brick that broke a window.

"Was the brick as big as my two fists?" asked the judge.

"Bane bigger."

"As big as my head?"

" 'Bout as long but not so thick."

———————

The judge glowered on the prisoner standing before him. The customary "Have you anything to say before sentence is passed?" was delivered with the proper inflection.

"Just this, your honor. I'm not an habitual criminal. This is only the second offense I've ever been charged with. And you know quite well my first conviction was wrong."

"Why should I know that?"

"Because you defended me."

So who wants to be a judge?

Every lawyer in your state.

———————

At a dinner party one night in the home of Judge Charles "Percy" Hutchinson, a guest looked across the table at his honor. "Judge," she cooed, "have you tried one of those new super-zombie cocktails? One-third absinthe, one-third cognac, and one-third rum."

"No," replied Judge Hutchinson, "but I've tried some who have."

———————

George Weiss, the general manager of the New York Yankee Baseball Club, spotted a rookie one day in spring training. "You look good out there, kid. What's your name?"

"Andrivividos."

"H'm. Kinda long. What's your nickname?"

"The boys call me Judge, Mr. Weiss, because I've sat on the bench so long."

------

The late Judge Jim Dolan was a noted wit in the court over which he presided in Jersey City. One prisoner before him told the usual story. He needed money to impress his girl friend. That's why he embezzled small sums of money.

"I understand," said Judge Dolan, "you were torn between love and booty."

On another occasion he asked a prisoner, "It says here you pick pockets. Kind of choosey, aren't you?"

But the prisoner, too, was snappy on the comeback. When Judge Dolan asked him, "How many times have you been here in this court?" the prisoner snarled, "Whatta yer expect me ter be, both a pickpocket and a scorekeeper?"

------

Judge Miles D. Coughlin, of Nevada City, California, was holding a session in city court when there was considerable noise in the rear of the room. The judge spoke to his bailiff. "I don't want levity in my courtroom."

The bailiff hurried to the rear and ejected the man causing the disturbance. Then advancing to the bench he spoke to Judge Coughlin. "You'll have no more trouble from Levity. I just tossed him outside."

------

Judge Al Cooper has had his problems in the Trenton, New Jersey, police court.

He asked a prisoner the usual question. "How do you plead? Guilty or not guilty?"

"Not guilty."

"Ever been in court before?"

"No, Judge. This is the first time I ever stole anything."

The judge repressed a smile. But the courtroom was engulfed in laughter. Judge Cooper gently rapped his gavel. "Order, please. Order."

The prisoner, still bewildered, looked up and said, "I'll take ham on rye."

———•—•———

No one ever challenged Federal Judge Meaney without a resultant fight. A lawyer stepped before him one morning and said, "The defendant refuses to leave New York and appear before this tribunal. He is living at the Ritz."

Judge Meaney reached for paper and pen. "Be patient, Counsellor. He'll leave the Ritz when these writs are served on him."

———•—•———

"May I plead, Judge, for a suspended sentence for my client?" orated counsel for defense. "After all, there are extenuating circumstances behind this homicide."

The judge toyed with his tortoise-shell glasses. "A suspended sentence? Yes, I think that's just what I'll give the defendant. I sentence him to be hanged on the morning of February 18th."

———•—•———

"Have you ever been up before me?"
The prisoner did not budge.
He looked at the court and made this retort—
"What time do you get up, Judge?"

———•—•———

The previous mention of a suspended sentence recalls the story of Bob Purvis, of Mississippi. The late Bob Ripley revived it at a dinner in Philadelphia. "Purvis," said Ripley, "will tell his story on my radio program next Sunday night. He was convicted in Mississippi of murder and sentenced to be hung. Something went wrong with the mechanism and Purvis was returned to his cell. While waiting, the Supreme Court of Mississippi gave him a new trial. Later the real murderer was caught and confessed the crime. Purvis, with the noose around his neck, was as close to death as any man could be. He settled down in a little town in Mississippi, married a lovely girl, and became the father of eleven husky youngsters."

The toastmaster looked at Ripley. "This chap, Purvis, who was almost hung, became the father of eleven children. Is that right, Bob?"

"Yes," said Ripley.

The toastmaster smiled. "I'd say the guy was well hung."

———•·•———

Watson B. Berry knew a Supreme Court judge who had relinquished a lucrative practice to go on the bench. One evening at dinner, a wealthy friend said to the new judge: "It puzzles me how you can pass up your practice for the low salary of a Supreme Court judge. It costs me twice that to live."

The judge smiled caustically. "I wouldn't pay it, Harry. It isn't worth it."

———•·•———

One of the best stories emanating from Senator Ed Ford, Harry Hershfield, and Joe Laurie of "Can You Top This?" was the tale of the judge suffering temporary "mental languish" as he gazed down on the habitual criminal.

"Seems to me," said the judge wearily, "that you've been coming up before me for the last twenty years."

The prisoner looked up petulantly. "Can I help it, Judge, if you don't get promoted?"

# CHAPTER 4

# "The Whole Truth
# —and Nothing Like the Truth"

AN OLD COUNTRY editor once remarked, "Many a man with a clear conscience has really only a poor memory."

To obtain the thorough understanding of memory—good or poor—you merely have to visit the nearest courtroom when the witness is sworn in. Judge Blair at a dinner one evening stated, "The two incumbrances to justice under our system of jurisprudence are the witness who starts off with . . . 'It appears' . . . and what we euphemistically term a jury of our peers."

"With men," says Gelett Burgess, "a lie is a last resort. With women, it's a first aid. With a woman, a lie is not a form of moral turpitude, but just a convenient little thing, like a hairpin. No woman, apparently, is ever in the least fooled by other women's lies." Perhaps that is why we have today so many women jurors.

Pope well knew how speech may be distorted when he wrote:

> The flying rumours gather'd as they roll'd,
> Scarce any tale was sooner heard than told;
> And all who told it added something new,
> And all who heard it made enlargements too.
> In every ear it spread, on every tongue it grew.

Now take the spinster that James Whitcomb Riley tells about. She was in the witness box and was grumbling at the question, "How old are you?" She sparred with the judge; she tilted with counsel.

"Hurry up, madam," advised the judge. "Every minute makes it worse, you know."

———————•◆—————

No one typifies the average witness more than the sweet young lady when she was sworn in. "Yes," she warbled, "I'll tell the truth, the whole truth, and nothing *like* the truth."

It is this characteristic in the lady witness, her unpredictability, that makes the cross-examining lawyer so chary.

Once in a New York court, the defense counsel thought he was asking a friendly, but informative, question. He spoke to the Irish witness. "Did you say, Mrs. Thompson, that you heard the sound of the three blows?"

"Oh, thim blows," she replied. "Oh, thim terrible blows, is it? I could hear the villain as he laid them on with his club. I could hear the poor creature groanin' and sufferin'. 'Twas awful, thim moans. 'Angels and saints, have mercy on her,' says I."

The defense counsel wanted no such testimony in the record if he could help it. He pleaded with the witness. "Stop, stop. You could have answered my question with a simple 'Yes.'"

She took up the cudgels. "Stop, is it? Yer can't stop me till I've had me say. I swore to tell the truth and, by God, I will. I heard her moanin' and I said to my daughter, 'The brutal baste is murderin' the poor soul, run out and get a cop.'"

Again defense counsel was on his feet. "I object, your honor—"

"Object?" She again took up her cudgels. "Sure yer would have objected if yer'd heard thim terrible blows that kilt her

. . . the poor sufferin' crature, so sweet she was, too. I hope he gets all that's comin' to him, the bloodthirsty devil."

Another lady witness had a problem, too. She leaned over to his honor. "Judge, may I correct my testimony? A few minutes ago I was so flustered at this, my first appearance as a witness, that when the lawyer asked my age, I gave my bust measurement."

*"I was so flustered that when the lawyer asked my age I gave my bust measurement."*

A judge in Milwaukee once challenged the testimony of a witness. "Your honor," bristled the man, "I have been wedded to the truth since infancy."

The judge smiled. "Is the court to infer you are now a widower?"

———•—•———

The murder trial was nearing its climax. On the witness stand was a beautiful blonde. The prosecuting attorney glared at her.

"I'll repeat my question," he thundered. "Where were you on the night of October 13th?"

The witness hung her head. "Oh, please don't ask me that," she murmured. "I can't tell you."

The prosecutor stiffened. "You must tell us," he roared. "Stop stalling. Where were you on the night of October 13th?"

The beautiful damsel blushed. "All right," she assented finally. "If you must know, I'll tell you. I was at home, working out a crossword puzzle."

The prosecutor's eyes almost popped from his head. "Is that anything to be ashamed of?"

The blonde hung her head still lower. "Certainly it is," she sobbed. "A beautiful girl like me, wasting a night on a crossword puzzle."

———•—•———

Then there was the sultry, sloe-eyed beauty, seated in the witness chair, displaying plenty of "cheesecake," as depicted by Ben Roth in an inimitable cartoon.

While the D.A. seems perturbed, the dame looks up at the judge. "Move your chair a little closer, your honor. This is going to be good."

———•—•———

Women are consistent in their own way. A court clerk in Sacramento, California, reports that she got a 'phone call

from a woman who wanted advice on the appropriate thing
to wear when she appeared to pay a traffic fine.

Perhaps it was the same woman who was asked by an
Oakland judge, "Have you ever appeared as a witness in this
suit before?"

She was horrified. "Oh, no, Judge. The last time I testified
I wore my pin-striped, gray flannel suit."

———— • ————

The reason it takes so long to try a case in court is not the
long speeches the lawyers make, but the fact that it takes so
much time to explain what the lawyers are talkin' about.

Grandpa Snazzy was once called as a witness. The lawyer
said, "Now, Mr. Snazzy, did you or did you not, on the date
in question or at any time previously or subsequently, say or
even intimate to the defendant or anyone else, whether
friend or mere acquaintance or in fact a stranger, that the
statement imputed to you, whether just or unjust and denied
by the plaintiff, was a matter of no moment or otherwise?
Answer—did you or did you not?"

Grandpa thought a while and then said, "Did I or did
I not what?"

———— • ————

One witness in an automobile accident case stumped the
police judge who was booking the man in a preliminary
hearing. There had been the suspicion of drunken driving
and the judge was getting at the facts. "Did you pay any
attention to Officer Christiansen's whistle?"

"Attention?"

"Yes," said the judge. "Surely you know what attention
means, don't you?"

"Of course, I do. According to James, attention means the
mind taking possession in clear and vivid form one of several simultaneously possible trains of thought. Focalization
and concentration of consciousness are the essence of atten-

*"Have I appeared as a witness in this suit before? Oh, no, the last time I testified I wore my pin-striped, gray flannel suit."*

tion. It means withdrawal from diversion to deal effectively with the precise object. Now, Judge, can you repeat that after me?"

———•—•———

Paul Smith, of Adirondack Hotel fame, had a lawsuit involving a title to some property. When he walked into the courtroom in Malone, New York, his opponent came over to him. "Paul, are those your witnesses sitting over there?"

"They are," said Smith.

"Then you win," said the other. "I've used them witnesses twice myself."

———•—•———

A Pennsylvania coal miner was being sworn in during a court action. His hands were jet black.

"Take off your gloves," roared the judge.

"And you, Judge," said the coal miner, "put on your eyeglasses."

———•—•———

The witness was being cross-examined and the lawyer was asking the same question again and again. Everyone grew impatient, the witness particularly so.

"You say that after the auto passed, you saw the victim lying there in the street with his scalp bleeding?"

"Yes, I did."

"After the auto passed?"

"Yes."

"But did the car hit him?"

"Yes."

"Are you sure?"

"No. What I said was a lie. The driver leaned out and bit him as the car went by."

———•—•———

"Hold up your right hand and swear to tell the truth—" said the bailiff.

But the prisoner raised his left hand. "I said your right hand."

The prisoner looked at the judge. "Your honor, if you want the truth . . . I'm lefthanded."

———•———

A garrulous and determined woman was a witness in a murder trial. "I'd like to tell the story in my own way," she complained to the judge, "without the constant interruption of that slick-looking shyster—"

"Just a moment, madam," warned the judge. "The court will not tolerate such derogations. You mean the attorney for the defendant."

"I'm sorry, Judge," she apologized, "I only want to tell what I saw without being halted every minute by that—" Here she appealed to the judge—"Excuse me, your honor, what was the gorgeous title you gave that slick-looking shyster?"

———•———

Yes, the lady has the last word. Take Bessie, for example. The judge was tired of seeing the same woman before him on the same charges.

"Looking at your record, Bessie," he said sharply, "it appears that you have been before me and convicted thirty-five times for petty stealing."

"I guess that's about right, your honor," said Bessie sadly; then brightening, she added, "None of us is perfect."

———•———

There are other feminine prerogatives, of course, and they continually bob up in the witness chair. An attorney in Galveston was summing up. "Ladies and gentlemen of the jury, is not this a time for compassion? My client, now a widow through the negligence of the railroad, at the tender age of twenty-nine must now wage a courageous fight against the travails of the future . . ."

He felt a tugging at his sleeve. His client was whispering to him. "Not twenty-nine—twenty-four."

Then William H. Ellis tells us that Judge Emmett Perry, president of the National Council of Juvenile Court Judges, in trying a case in his home town of Birmingham, was speaking to a talkative woman witness.

"Now, Jane, you can't tell what your daughter told you for she is now dead and you can't testify to what a dead person said."

The witness: "Yes, Judge, but she wasn't dead when she told me that . . ." And the witness continued to tell what the deceased had told her.

Exhibit 3 of this series gives us other insights into female psychology.

A conscientious saleswoman in a downtown department store was on the witness stand. The prosecuting attorney asked her if the woman sitting in the courtroom was the one who had written a worthless check.

"The woman who wrote the check was dressed differently and wore her hair differently," the saleswoman said cautiously. Then, to the dismay of the defense attorney, the accused spoke up, "That's not true. I wore my hair the same way that day."

That was enough for the jury.

———•••———

Nothing exasperates the judge more than the incoherent witness. A jurist in Philadelphia tossed in the towel after this experience. He was sitting in a disputed paternity case and this time, like the situation in Philip Wylie's *Finnley Wren,* there were twins.

"Twins?" the judge looked surprised.

"Yes, sir," replied the mother. "Both boys."

"How do you tell them apart?" asked the judge, taking a kindly interest in the case.

"This one," said the mother, pointing, "is this and that one is that one there."

"Decidedly coherent, madam. But"—here the judge pointed—"might not this one be this also?"

"It might," said the mother. "Then, of course, that one would be that."

The judge should have pursued another line of inquiry, but he was now deep in the matter. "How do you manage to separate them?"

The mother explained. "We seldom do. But when we want to, we put one in one room and the other twin in another room."

"How do you know which one you're putting in each room?"

"We look and see which is in the other room and then we know the other is in the other room."

The judge refused to surrender. "But if one of them was in the house and the other was away somewhere, would you be able to tell which was in the house?"

"Oh, yes," said the mother, earnestly. "All we would have to do would be to look at him and then we would know the one we saw was the one in the house and then, of course, the one away somewhere would be the other. There are only two of them, you see, which makes it easy."

"Yes," wailed the judge. "If they were quintuplets I'd now be on my psychiatrist's couch."

———

Some years ago Notre Dame's star center, Frankie Szymanski, appeared in a South Bend court as a witness in a civil suit. "Are you on the Notre Dame football team this year?" queried the judge.

"Yes, your honor."

"What position?"

"Center, your honor."

"How good a center?"

Szymanski squirmed in his chair, but in confident tones admitted, "Sir, I'm the best center Notre Dame ever had."

Coach Frank Leahy, who was in the courtroom, was surprised, because the lad had always been modest and unassuming. When proceedings were adjourned, the coach asked him why he had made such a statement. Szymanski blushed. "I hated to do it, coach," he explained, "but after all, I was under oath."

———•◆•———

A witness in Augusta, Maine, was extremely nervous. He stammered and sputtered in answer to the very first question. "S . . . s . . . s . . . s . . . ssss . . . ssss . . ."

The judge was irate. He looked down at the arresting officer. "What's this man charged with?"

The officer smiled. "Sounds like carbonated water."

The next case was that of a Chinaman. He knew his rights. "I refuse to be sworn as a witness, Judge. I do not know your God. I am a Chinese."

"Swear him, anyway," ordered the judge. "Let's have no more Confucian."

———•◆•———

Judge W. O. Murray, of San Antonio, Texas, described the courtroom antics of a country lawyer, John T. Bevins, of Pearsall, Texas. Once Bevins was pleading for a continuance of a case because two witnesses had not appeared.

The judge interrupted him. "Your witnesses have just entered the courtroom."

"Then, your honor, may I still apply for a continuance on the grounds of surprise? Both of these rascals promised me they wouldn't appear."

———•◆•———

The judge was perturbed by the witness. "Don't use that word, lie. It has horrid connotations."

"What should I say?" asked the witness.

"As Robert Browning phrased it," suggested the jurist, "you might say that he fell from truth while climbing toward it."

———•———

A witness in another case had been examined by the plaintiff's lawyer and was turned over to the lawyer for the defense for cross-examination.

"Now, then, Mr. Smith," began the legal one, "what did I understand you to say that your occupation is?"

"I am a piano finisher," answered the witness.

"Yes, I see," persisted the lawyer, "but you must be more definite. Do you polish them or move them?"

Bennett Robbins used the same staccato touch when he was told that the other side rested and he might begin his cross-examination. Mr. Robbins' client had charged the defendant with alienation of wifely affections.

"Mr. Zebruggi, what is your occupation?"

"I am in the house-wrecking business," answered the defendant.

"That will be all," said Mr. Robbins, with a sagacious look at the jury.

———•———

"You are lying so clumsily," said another judge to a witness, "that I would advise you to get a lawyer."

———•———

"Are you guilty or not guilty?" asked the police magistrate.

"Now that," said the prisoner, "is difficult to answer. Isn't that the very thing we are trying to find out?"

———•———

Sir Henry Irving was once a witness in the case of a street robbery. The thief's lawyer roared at the distinguished actor: "At what hour did the theft occur?"

"I think—" began Sir Henry.

The lawyer interrupted. "It isn't what you *think* that we want to know."

"Well, then, I might as well leave, because I'm not a lawyer—I can't talk without thinking."

A witness in a case in Cleveland had an experience similar to Sir Henry's. He asked the court's assistance. "Judge, I don't know what to do."

The judge was puzzled. "What do you mean by that statement?"

*"I swore to tell the truth, but every time I try some lawyer objects."*

"I swore to tell the truth," said the witness, "but every time I try, some lawyer objects."

———•—•———

Frank P. McCarthy, the jovial Jersey lawyer, has a collection of statements given by witnesses in various actions. We cull the following:

I've met this man, Counsellor, in places where any decent person would be ashamed to be seen.

Do I know him? I'll say I do. He's as cold as a dog's nose and as mysterious as chop suey.

I don't want to say anything against him, Judge, but if I were a chicken I'd roost high until he passed by.

I wouldn't exactly say he is a liar. But when it comes time to feed his hogs, he has to get somebody else to call 'em for him.

He uses statistics as a drunken man uses a lamppost. For support rather than illumination.

Reputation for honesty? I'd say Jed is as straight as one of them thar scenic railways in an amusement park.

———•—•———

Before Judge Edward Weil in the Magistrate's Court, New York, a young man appeared as a witness for the defense.

Judge Weil thought he recognized a familiar face. "Have you ever been convicted of a crime?" he asked.

The witness was truthful. "Yes, your honor. I was guilty of disorderly conduct."

"And what was the nature of the disorderly conduct?" The witness was hesitant. "Judge, it was . . . uh . . . disorderly conduct . . . rape."

———•—•———

George Clark, the venerable and lamented reporter on the Jersey *Journal,* covered the Fifth Precinct Station in Jersey City. He noticed that Sergeant Barry always made a cryptic notation on the police blotter when certain malefactors were brought in. The sergeant scribbled *S and B* after the culprit's name.

One night George asked the sergeant, "What does *S and B* stand for?"

The sergeant told him. "Salt and battery."

———•—•———

W. E. Nesbitt, of Columbia, Tennessee, reports a similar case. The defendant reared up when he heard the charge lodged against him. "Judge, that's a lie. I didn't put any salt in his battery. I merely wanted to knock his head off."

———•—•———

Truth is the important ingredient of any legal issue. It's always on the judge's mind and even when he sat in the dentist chair, he asked for verification. "Is the tooth out?"

"Yes," responded the dentist. "The tooth, the whole tooth, and nothing but the tooth."

The judge knows that truth is something that can always be sacrificed for expediency, however. He watches every witness carefully for the slightest deviation from fact. In one case the holier-than-thou attitude of the witness annoyed the judge. The witness was spouting off. "I was never caned but once in my life and that was for speaking the truth."

The judge grunted. "Probably cured you."

———•—•———

Charles J. Nichols, of Portland, Maine, knows the peculiar stories witnesses tell. This is his contribution to the Propagation of Truth in our Courtrooms.

The county attorney had presented members of the police force and other witnesses to identify the property as stolen, and establish that the respondent knew it was at the time of taking it into his possession, then rested the case. The attorney for respondent arose and called upon his client to take the stand with these words:

"Now, Mr. L——, go right around where that rail is and

tell the jury all that you know and all that you do not know about this case."

The judge interrupted: "How is he going to tell all that he does not know about the case?"

The attorney quickly replied, "Your honor, that is what the witnesses for the other side have been doing."

———•———

Another judge in Portland, Oregon, was becoming impatient at the witness for continually stating things against the evidence. "I hope you remember," he cautioned the man, "that you have sworn to tell the truth."

"Yes, sir, I remember."

"And do you know what to expect if you don't tell the truth?"

"Yes, Judge, I expect to win the case."

———•———

Two cab drivers met. "Hey, pal," asked one, "whatsa big idea? How come your cab's painted red on one side and blue on the other?"

"Bub," was the answer, "it's a riot. When I gets in an accident you should hear how all the witnesses contradict each other."

———•———

And what of the lad of doubtful age who entered the witness box?

"Are you an adult?" asked the judge.

"Am I? I'm the most adulterous man on Jackson Avenue."

———•———

There are witnesses in other than court actions. This chap was before the Sugar Rationing Board. "My wife has no sugar at all in our house—not an ounce!" The chairman of the board warned him. "Remember, you are swearing to this. You must tell the truth or you'll go to jail." The chap thought for a moment. "Gotta tell the truth, eh? In that case, rather than do a stretch in jail, I'll tell you. We ain't married!"

---

After weeks of patient effort the psychiatrist finally diagnosed the great lawyer's neurosis. "I had Dr. Enright, the eminent authority on forensic medicine, against me in the case," said the lawyer. "All that the court would allow me was a hypothetical question."

"Yes, yes, go on," said the psychiatrist, soothingly.

"Our office worked on the question for weeks. We checked all possible answers against the most authoritative medical opinion. It took me one full hour to ask the question."

"Yes, yes, go on," cooed the psychiatrist.

"And then when I had finished . . ."

"Yes?"

"The witness asked me . . ."

"Yes?"

"If I would mind repeating the question."

---

Children, too, can be a problem for the cross-examiner. As Jules Tepper used to say, "Get the kids on quickly and get 'em off quicker."

A boy who was a witness in court was asked by a lawyer: "Did anyone tell you what to say in court?"

"Yes, sir."

"I thought so. Who was it?"

"My father, sir."

"And what did he tell you?"

"He said the lawyers would try to get me all tangled up, but if I stuck to the truth, I would be all right."

---

The cross-examiner has always to be wary of what the late Justice Minturn called "folk testimony," those odd figures of speech used by ruralites. One lawyer in Georgia pressed for an answer to his question. "But you said my client was lazy, didn't you?"

"Wall, now, Mr. Lawyer," said the witness, "Ah don' wan' to do the man an injustice. But aroun' these hyer parts we all know ef it required any voluntary and sustained exertion on his part to digest his food, he woulda died years ago from lack o' nourishment."

Up in Maine, a witness had used the odd phrase, a "non-possibility."

The lawyer jumped on him immediately. "Non-possibility, eh? Suppose you give the court and the jury an example of a non-possibility."

The witness was reluctant to talk. But the lawyer prodded him. "Well," said the backwoodsman, "it'd be a non-possibility to make your mouth any bigger without setting your ears further back."

———————•••———————

Sam Schlepperman was a witness in one of the Kenny Baker radio shows. The judge told Sam indignantly, "I'll just fine you now . . . but if this happens again tomorrow, I'll toss you in jail."

"I get it," said Sam. "Fine today . . . cooler tomorrow."

# CHAPTER 5

# *"Juries and Other Injuries"*

THERE IS only one thing that doesn't work right when it's fixed. And that's a jury. A jury, be it known, is comprised of twelve people chosen to decide which side has the better lawyer. When the jury system originated as a democratic institution, a staunch defense of the inherent rights of the submerged classes against their lords and masters, it involved a sacred principle. But it has become an unbelievable waste of time. The juror reports at ten in the morning. The roll is called and the calendars are made up. Lawyers argue for delay; witnesses have left for the Coast. The jury hangs around even before they're hung up.

Some states, notably New Jersey, have speeded up the judicial processes so that the judge no longer disappears into his chambers to finish his crossword puzzle or discuss the stupidity of the appellate court in reversing him in Gafoozus vs. Hinkledinkle. Juries don't twiddle their thumbs waiting for justice to triumph over extended luncheon periods and protracted delays.

What makes our jury system unfathomable is the insistence on an unanimous verdict if Slugger Maloney bashes in the jutting jaw of George the Gimp, whereas the United States Supreme Court determines the constitutionality of our enacted laws by a five-to-four decision.

Who can explain, too, the lawyers' insistence on ignorance as the proper qualification of a juror?

"Ever serve on a jury?" asked a judge of a prospective panel member.

"No, I've been too smart to get caught on a jury."

The judge exploded. "What's that? Do you boast of your smartness in escaping jury duty? Why, this is the highest expression of good citizenship."

"No, sir," explained the man. "I meant I was always excused because the lawyers thought I wasn't ignorant enough."

---

The less ability the prospective juror has to form an intelligent opinion in the case, the more acceptable he is. Cognizant of this was Maurice Fogel of London. He tried, unsuccessfully, to be excused from registering for jury duty on the grounds that he was a professional mind reader. He might embarrass the court once the trial got under way.

And what of lady jurors? Generally speaking, a lady is generally speaking. What happens when she has to do all the listening? And suppose the lady defendant is wearing the same dress or hat as a woman juror? Can we expect an impartial verdict?

The first jury of twelve women, exclusively, sat in a case involving another woman before His Majesty's Justice of the Peace in Accomac, Virginia, on March 18, 1679. Not having a transcript of the case, we indulge in a brief flight of fancy to picture the reactions of such a female jury studying one of their own sex.

Juror Number One: "She looks guilty to me."

Juror Number Two: "To me, too. Look at the way she does her hair."

Juror Number Three: "Her husband seems so mild."

Juror Number Four: "Why she would caress his cranium

with a club is beyond me unless you notice that cruel look
in her eye."

Juror Number Five: "Isn't that a new Paris style she's
wearing?"

Juror Number Six: "It sure is. Makes you wonder where
she gets the money unless—"

Juror Number Seven: "Oh, I don't know. She looks the
type to me."

Juror Number Eight: "She doesn't act repentant."

Juror Number Nine: "Too cold-blooded."

Juror Number Ten: "Could we send her to the gallows?"

Juror Number Eleven: "I think so."

Juror Number Twelve: "I suggest it."

The culprit is then sworn in and she tells her story to a
jury of her "jeers."

"His lordship's justice and ladies of the jury, why did I
bat in my husband's brains with a belayin' pin? Mine is a
simple story. Every Saturday night he compelled me to
bathe his body."

The court interrupted. "That does not seem, madam, a
reasonable incitation to mayhem."

"But last Saturday night when he came home, your honor,
he was clean."

The lady jurors nudged each other, retired, and came in
with a verdict of "Not guilty."

———•—•———

When Sir Thomas Noon Talfourd wrote "Fill the seats
of Justice with good men, not so absolute in goodness as to
forget what human frailty is," he unwittingly voiced the
theme of the jury fixer. One such slickeroo thought he had
everything arranged for the defendant in a prohibition case.
Slipping some money to Juror Number Four, the fixer
whispered, "It ain't much of a crime to run a speakeasy. Go
in there and convince the others."

But the prosecutor was John Drewen, of Hudson County, as incorruptible as Robespierre. He spoke feelingly, convincingly, to the jury about respect for our laws because, though sometimes objectionable, they were integral parts of our American system. The jury came in with a verdict of "Guilty."

The fixer promptly sought out Juror Number Four. "How come, pal, you take my money and yet you fall down on me?"

"I couldn't help it, Paddy. I was all for your man until John Drewen summed up. Paddy, he talks just like the parish priest."

In the play by George Kaufman and Moss Hart, *You Can't Take It With You,* an elderly character never paid his income tax simply because he didn't believe in it.

A woman in Bergen County, New Jersey, had similar ideas about our jury system. Answering a summons for jury duty, she wrote: "In answer to your letter, I am not interested in your offer. I have a good paying job now."

A Baltimore judge, disgusted with a jury that could not come to agreement in a perfectly clear case, arose and said, "I discharge this jury."

One juryman, angry at what he considered a rebuke, said, "You can't discharge me."

"And why not?" asked the surprised judge.

"Because," said the juror, pointing to the defense attorney, "I'm being hired by that man there."

Someone hired Clancy as Juror Number Seven to hold out for a disagreement on a murder charge.

When the jury filed in and the foreman announced: "We cannot reach an agreement," the fixer was overjoyed. He rushed to Clancy's side and pumped his hand. "Was it much of a fight in there?" asked the fixer.

"It sure was," said Clancy. "The other eleven wanted to acquit the guy but I held out for the disagreement."

———•—•———

The prisoner, accused of a serious crime, had no lawyer. "This is a very serious offense you are charged with," the judge said. "Have you no counsel to represent you?"

"No, your honor," said the prisoner. Then he leaned confidentially toward the judge and said, "But I have some very good friends on the jury."

———•—•———

The prosecuting attorney in Houston, Texas, was having trouble with an evasive witness. Finally he asked him if he was acquainted with any of the members of the jury.

"Yes, sir," replied the witness, "with more than half of them."

"Are you willing to swear that you know more than half of them?" the lawyer demanded.

"If it comes to that," the witness replied, "I am willing to swear that I know more than all of 'em put together."

———•—•———

M. Neal Smith, of Longview, Texas, describes the prejudice of local citizens against that form of robbery known as "high-jacking." Knowing that this feeling lessened a juror's impartiality, the lawyer representing a defendant accused of such a crime challenged one of the jurors on this point. "Would you have a prejudice against a man accused of high-jacking?" The prospective juror said he would. After a few more questions he was turned over to the district attorney for further questioning. The district attorney attempted to show that this juror had no more prejudice against the offense of robbery than against any other offense. He asked the prospective juror this question: "Mr. Jones, you said a minute ago that you were prejudiced against a person charged with high-jacking. Now, Mr. Jones, you have no more prejudice against a person charged with the offense of high-jacking than you would if he were charged with any other offense equally as serious, for instance, rape, would you?"

"Yes, Mr. Erisman, I would," said the juror.

Whereupon the district attorney interrogated him further, "Now, Mr. Jones, if that is true, tell the court why you would be more prejudiced against a person charged with high-jacking than you would a person charged with rape." To which question the prospective juror replied in all seriousness, "Why, Mr. Erisman, I am a lot more susceptible of being high-jacked."

———————

Tired of waiting an unreasonably long time for jury verdicts, an Oklahoma City judge had hard-seated chairs substituted for the comfortable ones in the jury room. Then he timed the jurymen and found that the time for reaching verdicts was reduced by an hour.

Deciding to keep up the good work, he had all the chairs removed and discovered that juries which had to stand while deliberating reached verdicts in even less time.

His final move reduced deliberation to a minimum: he had all the windows in the jury room nailed down so that the air became stale in a short time.

———————

This incident in Cincinnati might be called "The Case of the Missing Juror."

The bailiff called the judge's home. "I thought I had the jury locked up, your honor, but I've just discovered one of them is missing."

"I'll get dressed," said the judge, "and come right down."

The bailiff, meanwhile, after a strenuous search, located

the missing juror home in bed, snoring in full contentment. When haled before the judge the juror explained his strange conduct. "I only did what you told me, Judge," he said.

"What did I tell you?"

"You said the jury might retire for the night. So I went home and retired."

———— • • ————

The lawyer walked into court with his undersized Irish client.

"I think, Cassidy, we should challenge the jury."

Cassidy squinted an eye at the panel. "I'm not in fightin' condition, but I'm sure I could go five rounds with that little runt in the corner."

———— • • ————

Out west, where conviviality precedes convention and the rules of order make way for colloquial interjections, a lawyer opened up for his client.

After stressing his side of the story and before calling the first witness, he looked directly at the jury and asked the rhetorical question: "Could my client be guilty—is he guilty?"

The foreman chuckled. "He don't look it—but you do."

———— • • ————

A Union Pacific shopman, drawn for jury service, asked the judge to excuse him. "We are very busy at the shops," said he, "and I ought to be there."

"So you are one of those men who think the Union Pacific couldn't get along without you," said the judge.

"No, your honor," replied the shopman. "I know it could get along without me, but I don't want it to find out."

———— • • ————

The judge was interrupted by the foreman of the jury. "After listening to the plaintiff," said the foreman, "we are inclined to think that he is right, but now that we have heard the other side," he continued, "we believe the defendant is right."

The lawyers for the litigants were astonished. The judge gave his counsel. "It is not my business to interfere," he remarked, "but how is it possible for both to be right?"

"Well, now," replied the foreman, "it is perfectly evident that you, Judge, are right."

———•———

"I'd like to be excused from jury duty, Judge," said the neat, elderly man in a Rochester, New York, court. "I'm deaf in one ear."

"I'm sorry," answered the judge, "but you will have to serve. In this court we hear only one side of the case at a time."

———•———

Since he had never been in court before, the old fellow was naturally impressed by the solemn dignity of the proceedings, and especially by the judge. In answering the questions fired at him by the attorneys, he spoke directly to the judge, as if the two were holding a private conversation.

The judge ignored it for a time, as the old man was speaking loudly enough for the jury to hear. But finally the judge interrupted.

"Counsellor," he said to the old fellow's lawyer, "tell your witness to speak to the twelve jurymen."

The old man heard, struggled to his feet, and bowed reverently to the jury.

"Good morning, gentlemen, I'm powerful glad to meet you."

———•———

Whether a jury is a group of twelve people of average ignorance may be a moot point. But when it comes to tampering, it's another matter.

Because the jury at the first trial of Boss Tweed in New

York City in 1873 disagreed on a verdict, the prosecution
at the second trial made certain that it had at least twelve
"untouchable" jurors by assigning twelve officers to watch
them, twelve watchers to watch the officers, and twelve other
watchers to watch the watchers, all thirty-six of whom had
to report daily.

It was during the impaneling of a jury that the following
colloquy occurred. "You are a property holder?"

"Yes, your honor."

"Married or single?"

"I have been married for five years, your honor."

"Have you formed or expressed any opinion?"

"Not for five years, your honor."

Perhaps this might explain an occurrence in Springfield,
Illinois.

The judge looked at the all-female jury. "After twenty-
four hours you are unable to arrive at a verdict?"

"We have arrived at twelve verdicts, your honor."

The judge was patently angry with the jury that could
not reach a decision. In forceful language he excoriated their
lack of attention, their failure to grasp legal fundamentals,
etc.

One little old man in the rear of the jury box stood up.
"Please, Judge, don't be peeved at me. I'm the only one on
your side."

It was the first case tried in Stony Gulch, and the jury
had been arguing for hours. When at last they straggled
back, the foreman, a tall mountaineer, expressed the general
opinion.

"We don't think he done it," he drawled slowly, "for we

allow he wa'n't there; but we think he would've if he'd had the chanct."

———— ·—·—— ————

At a trial of a criminal case, when the prisoner entered a plea of "Not guilty," one of the jurymen at once stood up. The judge informed him that he could not leave until this case was tried.

"Tried!" repeated the juror, in astonishment. "Why, he confesses that he is not guilty."

———— ·—·—— ————

Another judge who was peeved, this time at the prisoner, was a jurist in a small county seat in Minnesota. The defendant was charged with grand larceny.

There was no doubt about his guilt, but there was some question about the value of the stolen merchandise. The wholesale cost of the groceries was $35 but they would retail for more than that in the store. This difference meant a term in the penitentiary or one in the local jail.

"I sentence the defendant to the penitentiary," said the judge. "Considering how he came by these groceries, I'll be damned if I'll let him have them wholesale."

# CHAPTER 6

# The Comedy of Eros

Who has the proper claim to the warm spot in bed on a cold night? The wife who braved the icy sheets or the husband who comes home later and demands the coveted place? Superior Court Judge Van Nostrand had this perplexing problem to decide some years ago in San Francisco. It was a divorce action between Mr. and Mrs. Jack Weisinger.

The police had been called to the Weisinger home to quell a torrid battle when Weisinger ordered his wife to move over and she, rightfully, insisted on remaining in the area that she had warmed. Of such events is the kingdom of divorce. And, as all lawyers agree, nothing is trivial when husband and wife square off at each other. Every event is important. You can't blame one party and absolve the other until you have all the facts. Take the classic quarrel of them all—that between Adam and Eve.

> It is not fair to visit all
> The blame on Eve for Adam's fall;
> The most Eve did was to display
> Contributory . . . negligee.

The only chap who has the right answer is the bachelor. Here is a guy who has lost the opportunity of making some woman miserable. He's a fellow who has been lucky in love. And he glories in it. He has no children . . . to speak of.

He can put his socks on from either end. And there are no cold spots in any bed as far as he is concerned. Yes . . .

> The bachelor's a cagey guy,
> And has a lot of fun;
> He sizes all the cuties up
> And never Mrs. one.

We have no way of knowing whether the only rift in the lute of Mr. Weisinger was his aversion to freezing his posterior. But from all the statistics available in the divorce courts, you can't satisfy the woman you're married to.

If you go away on a trip and forget to bring her back a present, she thinks you no longer love her. If you do bring back a present, she's suspicious.

If you come home late from the office and she asks what kept you and you tell her the truth, she doesn't believe you. If you tell her a lie, she finds it out.

If you come home full of pep and energy, she knows what you want. If you come home tired and listless, she thinks you've already had it. You just can't satisfy your spouse.

———•———

The alternative to domestic trouble is divorce or bigamy. The penalty for the latter is two mothers-in-law. A bigamist is a guy who has had one too many. There's no solution there. In fact, you can't win at all. If your intentions aren't serious, you run into the law. For . . .

> . . . men who drip with petty phrases
> Oft forget the legal phases.

If you start chasing any skirt, you may wind up with a suit on your hands. In this chapter we have plenty of exhibits.

First, there was the dentist who married the manicurist. Today they're fighting tooth and nail.

A Wisconsin wife told the court that the retired naval officer she married insisted that they sleep in a hammock. In twenty-three years of married life, she'd fallen out of the hammock sixteen times. "I'm not careless . . . I'm all callous," she moaned, "and the grounds I've been falling on seem sufficient for divorce."

A Los Angeles woman filed for divorce immediately after the wedding. She said she and her husband went directly from the altar to his favorite bar, where he said to the mixologist in the white apron, "Well, I told you I'd marry her. Pay me the five dollars."

Before the decisive step toward divorce is taken, there is always recourse to the sympathetic friend who is willing to share your great trouble just to hear about it. One lady in Brooklyn (applause from the audience, please) sought out her best girl friend and cried on her shoulder. "Aloysius is neglecting me. I'm afraid it's another woman."

"Nonsense," advised her friend. "You're just using the wrong technique. Any husband requires kindness and tolerance, not nagging and abuse. If he comes home plastered, what of it? Shrug it off by kindness."

"Thanks, Arabella, I'll try it."

The following night the husband came home in a spifflicated condition. The wife met him at the door, embraced him, and made him comfortable on the sofa. She brought his slippers and robe, hugged and kissed him, and told him how sweet he was. After an hour of this treatment, she said, "Honey, it's getting late. Let's go upstairs to bed."

"I might as well," he said. "I'll get hell when I get home anyway."

A wife in Stamford, Connecticut, thought she, too, detected the symptoms of boredom growing in her husband.

So she planned a weekend trip to New York, where at dinner, theatre, and nightclub she might rekindle the old feeling.

The couple registered at the Biltmore. Returning from their Saturday night junkets to a half dozen nightclubs, they entered the hotel suite. The husband had to be poured into bed, he was so lubricated.

The wife was worried about their two children. She reached for the 'phone to call the children's governess in Stamford, even though the hour was late. "Operator," she said, "I want Stamford 0-0-9-8-4-3-8."

The 'phone number jogged the somnolent memory of the husband. With Superman's strength, he raised himself on one elbow and pleaded, "Don't call that number, honey. Tha's ma wife."

———•—•———

What we believe is the greatest understatement ever yet spoken by a judge issued from the judicial mouth of an advisory master in a divorce action.

"To the wife," began this oracular opinion, "the imprisonment of her impecunious husband in jail might be temporarily gratifying. But in no other way can incarceration be useful to her."

———•—•———

"The feminine of bachelor?" The coed pondered the question during an examination. Then inspiration flashed. She answered, "Lady-in-waiting."

———•—•———

According to Judge Grey Anderson, of Galax, Virginia, a wife deserted by her husband, received from her departed mate the unconditional terms of his return:

> When the postman puts sand in the sugar
> And the milkman makes milk out of chalk,
> When the boys stay at home with their mother
> And the girls forget how to talk,

> And after a ball game is outlawed
> And the railroad runs under the sea,
> And the man in the moon
> Comes down in a balloon
> Then . . . you can come back to me.

---

There never will be a divorce in the home of a lady in California. She told her neighbors that her husband was going in for ethnology. She had found a ticket in his pocket for the fourth at Tanforan.

"What is this, dear?" she asked.

"It's a relic of a lost race," he said.

---

The Italian composer, Donizetti, claimed he wrote his best arias a few minutes after beating his wife.

Think of that the next time you hear *Lucia di Lammermoor.*

Alexandre Dumas, the father, had to knock his wife cold to create humor. He could write serious material without using mayhem. But when he needed a humorous mood, Mme. Dumas had to offer her features to his fist.

In other words, before he could finish *The Count of Monte Cristo,* she had to take the count.

---

Give a husband enough rope . . . and he'll skip.

One man who did skip heard about it later. This item appeared in the *American Legion Magazine*:

"If John Jones, who deserted my mother and me before I was born twenty years ago, will send me his present address, said bastard will proceed to kick his face in."

---

One of the American Bar Association's gifted humorists is counsellor Herman Distler, of Newark, New Jersey. He has a favorite story of the Jewish couple whose marriage was going on the rocks. In such cases, the couple often seeks out the advice of a rabbi.

The rabbi pleaded with them to patch up their quarrel, but they were adamant. "So," said the rabbi, "you know the consequences and you want to part. Remember this. You must divide your property equally."

The wife flared up. "You mean the $4,000 I have saved up? I must give him half? My money?"

"Yes," said the rabbi. "He gets $2,000. You get $2,000."

"What about my furniture? I paid for that."

"Same thing," answered the rabbi. "Your husband gets the bedroom and the living room; you get the dining room and the kitchen."

There was a challenging gleam in the wife's eye. "What about our three children?"

That stumped the rabbi. Shrewdly he assayed the situation, then, stroking his beard, he came up with a Solomonic answer. "Go back and live together until your fourth child is born. Then you take two children and your husband takes two."

The wife shook her head. "No, I'm sure, Rabbi, that wouldn't work out. If I depended on him, the schlemiel, I wouldn't have the three I got."

---

The average husband is proof enough that a woman can take a joke.

---

A lawyer in Boston looked hopelessly at his client, who was now behind the bars. "I can't figure it out," said the attorney. "One wife can be troublesome. Here you marry three of them at the same time. What prompted all this, Paul?"

"Oh," moaned Paul, "I just wanted to see if I could take it."

The other guy who chose bigamy to divorce was in a quandary. The judge glared down at him. "The jury having acquitted you of the charge of bigamy, you are free to leave the court and go home."

"Thanks, your honor," he said. "But I'd like to be on the safe side. Which home should I go to?"

---

"You meet some funny people in an office like this," commented a lawyer in Las Vegas. "One man who was here last month told me that he wanted a divorce after twenty-seven years of married life."

"'After twenty-seven years?' I asked.

"'Yeah,' he drawled. 'I know I should have come to you sooner.'"

The lawyer sat back in his chair. "Then one day a dame strolls in and says she wants to tie the can to papa. So I ask her politely what her charges are. Was I floored by her answer! She says, 'I thought I had to pay you.'"

---

Divorce lawyers have to employ a brand of salesmanship or risk the loss of a client. In Kansas City a man challenged the lawyer's fee. "You want to charge me $250 for a divorce? Why, it only cost ten dollars to get married!"

"But my dear fellow," explained the lawyer, "compare the relative benefits issuing from the respective services!"

---

The proposed divorce action called for a serious consultation between the lawyer and his fair client. "We'll need sufficient grounds," he said.

"What's that mean?"

"Proof that a divorce should be granted. For example, has he been cruel to you?"

"Only slightly."

"Deprived you of financial support?"

"No, I wouldn't say that."

"Of course, in this state we recognize adultery as sufficient grounds."

"You do?" she asked. A big smile spread over her face. "Oh, I can supply that."

*"Adultery is sufficient grounds? Oh, I can supply that."*

The newspapers portray an endless procession of the skirmishes that mark the battle of the sexes.

From Mexico City comes the story of Elena Morales, who reported to police that her husband first broke her left arm during a heated argument, then followed, when she fled to her mother's house, and broke her right arm.

In Texarkana, Arkansas, James W. Kimbrell, suing his fifteen-year-old wife for divorce, charged that she acted like a child.

A Des Moines woman seeking a divorce complained that her husband, although in perfect health, had gone to bed seven years before and was still there.

District Judge Horace D. Ballaine of Tulsa fretted over the custody of a car belonging to a couple awaiting their divorce. He finally awarded it to the husband for business, to the wife for weekend shopping.

———•———

Do coming events cast their shadows before? The wife stared at her husband. "What are you cutting out of the paper?"

"The story of a man obtaining a divorce because his wife searched his pockets."

She lowered one eyelid. "And what are you going to do with the clipping?"

"Put it in my pocket," he said.

———•———

Another couple faced the judge with the eternal problem.

"We were happy for over a year, your honor, and then— then Baby came."

"Boy or girl?"

"Girl—she was a blonde and moved in next door."

———•———

A New York lawyer, gazing idly out his window, saw a sight in an office across the street that made him rub his eyes and look again. Yes, there was no doubt about it. The pretty stenog was sitting upon the gentleman's lap. The lawyer read the name lettered on the window and then found it in the telephone book. Still keeping his eye on the man across the street, he called him up. In a few seconds he saw the man start violently and pick up the receiver.

"Yes," said the other through the 'phone.

"I should think you would start."

The victim whisked his arm from its former position and began to stammer something.

"Yes," continued the lawyer severely, "I think you'd better take that arm away. And while you're about it, as long as there seem to be plenty of chairs in the room—"

The victim brushed the young lady from his lap rather roughly.

"Who—who the devil is this, anyhow?" he managed to splutter.

"I," answered the lawyer, in a deep, impressive voice, "am your conscience."

———————

The uncertainty of the law was never more fully stated than in the case of an unlucky Englishman. He explained it all to a sympathetic friend. "My wife had me drawn into the divorce court. The main allegation? That I was sterile. Naturally, I engaged a solicitor to represent me. At the same time our upstairs maid went to Bow Street and lodged a paper against me, charging me with the fatherhood of her prospective baby. Again I had to engage a solicitor. And would you believe the uncertainty of the law? *I lost both cases.*"

———————

According to Jimmy Starr, author of *Heads You Lose* (Frederick Fell Inc., New York), a California judge said to the gay young divorcee, "H'm! Six husbands already! Seems to me you've developed a method of building a better spouse-trap than your neighbor."

*She's developed a method of building a better spouse-trap than her neighbor.*

The *Manchester Guardian* reported another case of a British home being menaced by female gallivanting.

A dignified Briton was taking home a pair of his wife's shoes which the shoemaker had repaired. As no wrapping had been supplied, because of the paper shortage, he was carrying them loose. A man opposite him on the bus who had watched him closely said, as he got out: "Not going to let her gad about—eh, guv'nor?"

We've mentioned bachelorhood as one of the certain evasions of marital difficulties. What about the spinster?

There is something to be said for this state of quiescence. The maid of a famous unmarried actress opined that it was a time of great mental repose "when you gave up struggling."

Another young lady had darkened views, too, about her hopes for marriage. She confided to one boy acquaintance, "I think I'll wind up an old maid."

He was a fresh young sprig, entirely uninhibited. He flexed his muscles. "I'd like to wind one up, too. Sounds like fun."

Her sister was a different type. She felt that marriage was worth any risk. She agreed with Mary Meyer that an ounce of suggestion was worth a pound of lure. So she quit high school in her fourth year . . . to get married. There was a girl who put her heart before the course.

———•———

One philosophical judge in Reno, summing up his years in a divorce court, gave this sage advice, "Experience is also a great preacher. In here I see everything. My one thought for all married couples is this: don't send your spouse to an early grave by a series of little digs."

———•———

Marital problems are not confined to the white race.

"See here," said the Indian inspector at a western reservation, "it is a violation of the law now to have more than one wife, and the law must be obeyed. When you get back home you tell all of your wives except one that they can no longer look upon you as their husband."

"You tell 'em," suggested the Indian, after a moment's reflection.

———•———

And, as for the colored brethren, well, just listen. Edison Marshall contributes this epic:

One morning Mose came to work with a black eye, a swollen lip and a jaw set in splints. His boss asked him what happened. "My wife," whispered Mose between his clenched teeth. "I was a-talkin' when I should have been a-listenin'."

What of Simeon Abercrombie Jones, being reprimanded for deserting his wife?

"Counsellor, ef you'd a knowed dat woman as Ah does, you wouldn't call me a deserter. Ah's a refugee."

*"Counsellor, ef you'd a knowed dat woman as Ah does, you wouldn't call me a deserter. Ah's a refugee."*

# CHAPTER 7

# The Ties That Blind

THE CLASSIC DICTUM of Ambrose Bierce that it was all right for a man "to fall into a woman's arms so long as he didn't fall into her hands" has plenty of refutation from the female side of the house. As one lady told a judge in Des Moines, "I was always having trouble with either my husband or the furnace, Judge. Every time I'd watch one, the other would go out."

Another dame in Madison, Wisconsin, added her comment to the divorce proceedings. "Why I married him, the Lord only knows. He had been turned down by so many girls that he looked like a bedspread."

The case for the ladies is well expressed in a parody by Mildred Plew Meigs in *Desk-Drawer Anthology*. The title is "Sonnet For Myself."

> When I reflect how good a wife I've been,
> How dutiful, domestic, and adoring,
> How unresponsive to the call of sin
> How circumspect and how completely boring;
> When I consider in my humdrum way
> How like to Cleopatra's past mine wasn't;
> How many mink and sable coats today
> Incline to white gardenias where mine doesn't;
> When I perceive how vice gets Packard Eights
> While virtue in the kitchen gets the dinner,

Despite my prudence and my predicates,
I wonder—as I view the saint, the sinner—

If time remains upon this mundane level,
To pack my trunk and hie me to the devil.

———•—•———

A Florida judge who has heard many divorce cases has some cryptic comments. He says that if couples planning marriage could only sit here with me for just one day, they would discover

(1) That alimony is the high cost of leaving.
(2) That understanding each other's failings, rather than developing "hardening of the hearteries," is the true solution for happiness.
(3) That divorce is one man's mate and another man's poison.
(4) Divorce is hash made of domestic scraps.
(5) Merely transposing the letter "I" can turn the *marital* relationship into a *martial* one.

Yes, and the judge might well add that divorce suits are always pressed with the seamy side out. In the beginning the girl looks at the boy and the feeling is nuptial. It takes two to make a marriage—the girl and her anxious mother. And if the admiration is sincere, not "make be-loving," the boy and girl are married for better or for worse, but not for good. Because, as the case histories of every divorce courtroom reveal, little quarrels grow into extended ones.

One man in Chicago who didn't kiss his wife in five years, shot a man who did. The wife may compare her husband with Farley Granger . . . and prefer Farley. The husband wants to argue with the wife, but every time he does, words flail him.

At this time, only Seneca's advice may keep the couple from the divorce court: "Shame may restrain what the law does not prohibit." But there's always a breaking point. Usually it is when the lady can't take any more and she breaks a chair over his head. Enters alimony. That's a man's cash surrender value, a contraction of the three words "all his money."

Before the divorce courts are reached, there are always preliminary steps. It is the snide remark, the coming home late for dinner, the reading of the baseball scores across the breakfast table. In one case the preliminary phases puzzled a judge. "You say this man is charged with beating his wife with an oak leaf?"

"That's the charge."

"But what's so awful about a little thing like that?"

The bailiff looked at the complaint paper. "This oak leaf was from the dining room table."

And what of these two old friends who met? They hadn't seen each other in years.

"What kinda dame did you marry, Fred?"

"She's an angel, Harry."

"You're lucky. Mine's still living."

How do they handle this situation in Hollywood?

It was an important movie in the making. The whole production had stalled because of a difficulty with the script, and the delay was costing the studio thousands of dollars.

In the story, the husband had fallen out of love with his wife, and there was disagreement as to how this suggestion could best be conveyed to the audience.

The producers called in one high-salaried writer, who wrote four pages of beautiful dialogue, but that was too long. Then they called in another writer, who penned two pages of biting wordage, but that was also too long.

Finally, the producer had an inspiration. He called in a typewriter-tapper who'd been scripting for films for twenty-five years—long before celluloid had found its tongue. "It's a cinch," he said. "I'll show you how we'll do it."

And this is the way it appeared in the final shooting: the husband and wife were riding down in an elevator. On the sixth floor, a young girl entered the car—and the husband removed his hat.

Or the pre-divorce stage may take this turn. Artie Chokes, a thoroughly brow-beaten husband, dashed frantically into the fire house. "Chief," he called out, "my wife has run away again."

"So what?" asked the chief wearily. "Why tell us? Take your problem around to the police station."

"I did the last time she ran away," said Artie, "and they found her."

There was a lady who did take her troubles to the police station but then apparently changed her mind. A court clerk in Richmond, Virginia, reported that a woman, told to wait an hour for a pistol permit, had flounced out saying, "No, that would be too late. I guess I'll have to use a knife after all."

The plaintiff husband in his divorce action charged cruelty in general terms. The wife's lawyer asked for a bill of particulars, which usually is a humiliating and intimate recording of details that should be sacred to husband and wife.

The understanding judge began to read the pleadings. Before he had finished, his white cheeks were suffused in blushes. "Gentlemen," he chose his words carefully, "I think we'll try this case in chambers. Apparently, that is where this cause of action arose."

How may we end divorce? Paul Morris comes forward with a poetic suggestion:

> Hurray! I have found the solution!
> Yes, I've finally delved to the source.
> And now I can tell you that marriage
> Is the principal cause of divorce.

———•◆•———

What are some of the odd grounds for divorce as revealed by court records?

A Cleveland woman obtained a divorce after telling the court that her husband was so determined that she reduce that he put her on a water diet for eight days, and, to make sure that she kept to it, he took her to work with him.

A woman in Massachusetts sued for divorce after charging that her husband had thrown her parrot out of a window because it had told on him for coming home late.

In Corpus Christi, Texas, a woman was given a divorce after telling the judge that her husband shut off his hearing aid to keep from hearing her side of the argument.

Charging that he hurled a prickly cactus plant at her while she was in a stooping position, Mrs. John B. Crane won an uncontested divorce from her husband, a Harvard University instructor.

A Pasadena, California, woman filed for divorce on the grounds that her husband made her do her reading in a closet so that his slumbers would not be disturbed.

Because her husband shot tin cans off her head with a slingshot, a Connecticut wife was given her freedom.

In Los Angeles, Mary Magley got her divorce after testifying that her husband insisted on hanging photographs of his four ex-wives in their bedroom.

Not yet divorced is the man in Hollywood who recently married for the seventh time. To his present wife's displeasure, he has busts of his first six wives in the dining room.

# 104

If you think southern gallantry has faded from Dixie, you libel that land of chivalry. For proof we turn to the pages of the *Webster Progress,* a newspaper in Europa, Mississippi:

Stern-faced Judge Guynes grinned for the first time in several years, during a court session in Brookhaven last week. Defendant in a family-trouble trial was being cross-examined. He said he had found a man in the bedroom with his wife when he came home one night. "Did he say anything when you found him there?" asked the district attorney. Pausing a minute, the defendant replied: "He said, 'I think I better be going along.'"

———

Dorothy Parker, baroness of the *bon mot,* was once bored by a loquacious actress who hadn't had a part since Belasco died. "I just simply loathe the idea of leaving the theater," she gushed, "I'm so wedded to it."

"Then," retorted Dorothy, "why not sue it for nonsupport?"

———

Ilka Chase, the girl of many talents, was riffling through a trunk about a month or so after Natalie Schafer had married Ilka's ex-husband. Discovering a box of calling cards of excellent texture and engraving, with "Mrs. Louis Calhern" embossed thereon, Ilka thought the cards should not be wasted. She mailed them to her successor.

Aware of Louis' well-known proclivity for shedding marital ties in whimsical moments, Ilka scrawled on one of the cards, "Dear Natalie, I hope these reach you in time."

———

A hard-boiled moll swayed her hips into a lawyer's office. "I want a divorce from Tommy the Trigger."

"Very well, madam," said the lawyer. "For the standard fees set by the Bar Association I can commence proceedings immediately."

"How much will it be?"

"Approximately three hundred dollars."

"Forget it," she said, as she started for the door. "I can have him bumped off for a hundred."

————•————

The unpredictable female! Here was her lawyer listening to an hour-long recital of marital abuses, ranging from

*"Three hundred bucks for a divorce? I can have him bumped off for a hundred."*

social embarrassments to third degree mayhem. "I've heard enough," said the lawyer. "You're entitled to a divorce. The guy is a brute. Someone ought to give him a taste of fisticuffs to see how he likes it." The lady arose.

"Why, where are you going?" asked the attorney.

"To consult another lawyer. I didn't come here to have Adolf abused."

———•◦•———

Harold J. Wilson, of Burlington, Iowa, grew poetic when he observed a divorce action filed under the names of LIEB versus LIEB:

> In Des Moines District Court
> A divorce suit was filed.
> Then because of the names
> The judge's clerk smiled.
>
> It was Lieb versus Lieb,
> Therefore LOVE was the title,
> But no love remained—
> See plaintiff's recital.
>
> There was smoking in bed
> By the visiting mother,
> While the husband complained
> His wife loved another.
>
> She often bought booze
> From the household exchequer,
> Leaving little for food,
> Even sandwich, one-decker.
>
> She wrote many checks
> On his bank account hoard,
> And now she spurns
> His bed and his board.
>
> No children were born
> Of such misfit relation.

So "lieb" meaning "love"—
Seems a faulty translation.

———•———•———

It's impossible for a woman to be married to the same man for fifty years, says Bernard Bailey.

After the first twenty-five—he's not the same man.

———•———•———

Pasquale Ansaldo, of Jersey City, owed twenty dollars to his estranged wife as a support allowance. The money was payable through the Hudson County Probation Bureau. Mr. Ansaldo didn't have the twenty dollars, so he walked into a Hoboken dress shop, flourished a gun at a lady employee and got twenty dollars exactly, which he took to Jersey City and turned over to the Probation Bureau for the account of his estranged wife.

The police got him very quickly and he was soon in jail. There was no difficulty about identifying him as the hold-up man. The lady he robbed to get the money to pay to his estranged wife was—his estranged wife!

———•———•———

Lily Schwamm, wife of the distinguished New York banker, served on a committee to welcome DP's (Displaced Persons). When she saw the boat docking at the New York pier, Mrs. Schwamm, hastening forward, noticed an elderly man and woman on the fringe of the arriving group.

Mrs. Schwamm called up to them. "I want you to come home with me for a few days." There were some whispered words and soon the old people were whisked up to the Schwamm home in Riverdale. After dinner, they were assigned to their room.

About an hour later, Mrs. Schwamm heard a timid step on the stairway. She saw the old lady. In splintered English, the elderly woman explained how grateful she was for all the kindness shown her but please, would Mrs. Schwamm explain one thing that was puzzling? "Who is this old man I'm supposed to sleep with? I never met him until today."

Tom Masson tells another quaint story in his collection, *Tom Masson's Annual* (Doubleday, Doran).

The Vicomte Sorigny, a distinguished member of the French Embassy, was present at the silver wedding celebration of a bishop. Leaning over to his neighbor, the bishop's nephew, the vicomte asked, *sotto voce:* "Tell me, what is this silver wedding which we celebrate? I do not quite understand."

"Oh," replied the bishop's nephew, "don't you know? Why, my uncle and aunt have lived together for twenty-five years without ever having been separated."

"Ah," exclaimed the diplomat heartily, a light breaking in upon his understanding, "and now he marry her? Br-ravo!"

In the Kentucky Circuit Court the judge asked what he thought was an innocuous question, "Have you ever been married, ma'am?"

The woman was hesitant. "Well, no, that is . . . not personally."

If the above sounds naïve, what about the woman in Holland, Michigan, who told the judge, "Your honor, all during my married life my husband spoke to me only three times."

The judge granted her the custody of her three children.

After a few words, mostly spoken by the young wife, her husband sprang to his feet.

"You've gone too far!" he exclaimed angrily. "This is our last quarrel. I'm going right out of your life."

"Oh, Henry, darling, where are you going?" she cried.

"Where I'll never trouble you again," he replied, as he started to open the door. "I'll find a place where wild adventure will wipe out the memories of this moment—perhaps in the jungle—or on the stormy seas . . ."

As he spoke he opened the door, then ducked in again, and turned sternly to his wife. "It's lucky for you that it's raining," he said.

———— •+• ————

For centuries the position of Arab women in North Africa was lowly. When traveling the man always rode the family donkey, while the woman carrying the household goods walked behind. But with the coming of war and the British and American troops, many customs changed. The man still rode the donkey but the woman was emancipated. She walked in front. There might be land mines!

———— •+• ————

John Zieck, an able-bodied truck driver of Kenosha, Wisconsin, turned to his wife in the tavern where they were having a few beers. "We've had enough. Come on home."

Mrs. Zieck argued she was not ready to leave. "You're coming," he said, "or I'm driving my truck right through this tavern." Mrs. Zieck wouldn't move.

Three minutes later Zieck crashed his ten-ton truck into the building. "Coming now?" he shouted. She shook her head and ordered another beer. Zieck backed up his truck and tried again. This time when he hit the building it collapsed. At that point, Mrs. Zieck decided to go home.

———— •+• ————

In Missouri, a housewife charged in her divorce suit that when she served steak and onions, her husband had his own ideas about sharing them: he ate the steak and left her the onions.

A Pittsburgh woman didn't consider her husband's attentions during an illness as being properly solicitous. She sought a divorce, charging that while she was ill her husband not only sent an undertaker to see her but ordered a brace of funeral wreaths.

In New Haven, Connecticut, a recently divorced man called the probation office to say he would not be downtown to make his weekly alimony payment, because "My wife took my shoes."

———— • • ————

The divorce trial was on and Schimsky was the defendant. So far as he was concerned, his wife could go jump in a lake. (He thought it was possible to marry both a beautiful girl and a good cook. Only a bigamist can do that.)

The judge was bitter. He raked Schimsky over the coals because the only defense seemed to be opposition to any alimony. "I don't care what you say, Mr. Schimsky. The court will see that your wife is paid seventy-five dollars weekly."

"Judge," said Schimsky, "you're such a good sport I'll tell you what I'll do. I'll throw in a coupla bucks a week myself."

Cicero, the great lawyer of Roman times, had a different opinion of Cleopatra than the Bard of Avon, who wrote of her . . .

> "Age cannot wither her, nor custom
> stale her infinite variety."

Cicero, seeing Cleo installed by Caesar in a magnificent villa outside Rome, said cryptically, "I can't abide the woman."

Not too long ago an old fellow came into the New York Bureau of Missing Persons and reported that his wife had been missing fifteen years. The bureau clerk was stunned. "You're just reporting it now? You want her back after all this time?"

The man nodded. "For years I couldn't abide her presence. But now my eyesight is failing, and it won't make much difference. She was always a good housekeeper."

———————

This story is reminiscent of one George Sanchez tells about the New York clubman who married the homeliest woman

*"I drag my wife around, Counsellor, because it's much easier than kissing her goodbye."*

in the city. He invariably escorted her to every cocktail party and theater he attended. A lawyer once asked him, "Why do you drag her around with you?"

The husband chuckled. "Counsellor, it's much easier than kissing her goodbye," he explained.

The Nevada State *Journal* reported the enterprise of one citizen anxious to get in a plug for local business. This man wrote to the Duke of Windsor at the time of his abdication from the English throne.

"Dear Sir:

"The world admires your courage in choosing a charming and beautiful life mate. If by chance the marriage is not successful, Reno, the world's divorce capital, will welcome you."

---

Love surely is wonderful. The judge looked down at the woman in Cheyenne, and said, "What makes you think your husband is getting tired of you?"

"He hasn't been home for seven years," she said.

---

We conclude this report of matrimony and its pitfalls by tabulating almost unbelievable events in the lives of certain married people:

The clerk of the Yuma, Arizona, Superior Court received a request from a Los Angeles man for a certified copy of a marriage license issued in 1939 to himself and "a lady whose name I have forgotten."

Judges of the Paris Divorce Court got a new one to figure out when a woman sued her husband for damages because she had had six children.

In Knoxville, Tennessee, Mrs. Elmore Fryar, suing for divorce, asked for her husband's motorcycle as alimony.

"While he never actually struck me," explained Sarah Sanders, suing Edward Sanders for divorce, "he would go around slamming his fist against doors and saying, 'I wish it was you.'"

William Wilson divorced his wife because she took his false teeth and held them for $2 ransom.

Testifying that her husband had knocked her out by hitting

her on the head with a live chicken and then, finding that the impact had killed the chicken, revived her and ordered her to cook it, Mrs. Viola Beck sued for divorce.

Ada Leonard, strip-tease dancer, filed suit for divorce because her husband, her attorney explained, "doesn't resent the fact that she is doing this kind of work. Is that clear?"

Samuel Hoffenstein, scenarist and poet of Hollywood, was divorced by his wife, who objected to the jingles he dedicated to her. We append an example:

> When you're away, I'm restless, lonely,
> Wretched, bored, dejected;
> But here's the rub, my darling dear,
> I feel the same when you are here.

# CHAPTER 8

# Police to Meet You

CRIME doesn't pay. You hear the theme reiterated over television and radio. The cinema, according to some of its defenders, exists only to expose sin. The pulp magazines reek with Dapper Dans boasting they have stolen millions and bumped off a few coppers in the interim. "But next Tuesday, I'm quittin'," said one of these.

"Why, Dan?" asked his roommate.

"That's the day I go to the chair."

But for every nine out of ten who have been enmeshed in the law, there is still a tenth who hasn't been given his legal pudding . . . or in other words, his just desserts.

Take the chap who appeared before Judge Jack Flaherty. "How do you explain that this man's wallet was found in your pocket?"

"Your honor," said Dextrous Dick, "life is a succession of inexplicable mysteries. I wish you would so instruct the jury."

Or take the plea of Counsellor Bill Moore, "My client, Judge, stole the ring only in a moment of weakness."

"I suppose," commented the judge, "if he'd had a moment of strength, he would have taken a safe."

There have been a great many miscarriages of justice. But the American Bar Association, through sub-committees, is constantly warring on legal loopholes. Charles F. French points this out quite plainly.

The highest court of a southern state in 1918 annulled a verdict and discharged a defendant because the indictment charged that he "did shoow" one Richard Armstrong, instead of shoot him. Oh, well, maybe the whole thing was a typographical error. Anyway, the victim "diew."

A man convicted of rape in the midwest was discharged after sentence had been pronounced upon him because a "the" had been left out of his indictment. A convicted murderer was freed because "did" was omitted from a 366-word indictment.

One Andrew Bryson was murdered. The death bullet was one of several fired from across a state line. The state where the trigger was pulled could not legally punish the murderers. The state where Bryson was struck could not reach them. Never having been there, they were not fugitives from the justice of that state.

But let us move on to our chronicle of other law evaders.

————————

When a felon's not engaged in his employment,
Or maturing his felonious little plans,
His capacity for innocent enjoyment
Is just as great as any honest man's.

That's the way W. S. Gilbert sums it up in *The Pirates of Penzance*.

Maybe the police eventually catch up with these culprits, but in the meantime they seem to enjoy life. Let's look at another exhibit.

A prizefighter and his lady dined at a large restaurant in the Times Square area. When the waiter presented the check, the prizefighter handed him a five dollar bill and told him to keep the change. The pug then got up and suddenly gave the waiter a black eye.

On the sidewalk, the fighter lighted a cigar. Then the police arrived.

"A fine waiter, that guy," the pug explained to the judge.
"I expect to dine there again tomorrow."

"If he's such a fine waiter," asked the judge, "why did you
slip him that black eye?" The pug puffed on his cigar. "I
like that guy for a waiter," he explained. "And when I go
back there tomorrow, I'll have no trouble picking him out."

Another malefactor the police didn't catch was the uniden-
tified culprit who tossed a brick into an Indianapolis
jewelry store window and scooped up a handful of rings.
What makes this episode eventful was the report of the
policeman. "Heard crash of glass at 11:15 P.M. Hurried to
scene. Saw man running away. He escaped. Returned to
scene. Found *that window was broken on both sides.*"

---

The classic example of "getting away with murder" was
the case of Lizzie Borden, of Fall River, Massachusetts.

Lizzie was a spinster tried for having bopped her ma and
pa, but a sentimental jury freed her because they couldn't
reconcile her position with murder. Lizzie was secretary of
the Young People's Christian Endeavor.

The humorists of those days told the story in doggerel:

> Lizzie Borden took an ax
> And gave her mother forty whacks.
> When she saw what she had done,
> She gave her father forty-one.

When Lizzie had retired to a life of bucolic contentment,
she would take long strolls in the woods. On the adjoining
farm was a little girl who loved to accompany Lizzie on
these peregrinations. The little girl's mother was horrified
when she heard of the acquaintance. She warned her child;
never again under any circumstances, was she to walk
through the woods with Miss Borden.

"Why, Mother?" asked the child.

The mother pondered what reason she should give. Then the bright light gleamed. "Once, darling, she was unkind to her mother and father."

———•—•———

The most popular man in the community killed a worthless fellow during a quarrel. Being an honest man, he pleaded guilty to first degree murder. It looked as if he would get the chair. But the jury, all friends of his, determined to save him in spite of himself. They brought in a verdict of not guilty.

"How in the world," said the judge, "can you bring in such a verdict when the defendant has pleaded guilty?"

"Well, your honor," said the foreman, "the defendant is such a liar that we can't believe him."

———•—•———

Jack Dempsey adds his recollections to our annals of crime.

Jemima Johnson had haled her ex-prize-fighter husband into court, charging him with constant wife-beating. Displaying a couple of cauliflower ears, a broken nose, lacerated mouth, and blackened eyes, she demanded that Rastus be punished.

"Rastus," said the judge, "you've heard what your wife testified. Have you anything to say?"

"Aw, Judge, don' pay no 'tenshun t' her," replied Rastus. "She's punch drunk!"

———•—•———

In the secret records of one of Chicago's robber bands is the story of one young gangster, quick on the trigger but slow in his mental processes, who was sent to look over a palatial home marked for a Christmas Eve looting job.

He crept silently through the shrubbery, looked into a drawing room, and saw a young lady and a young gentleman, both in evening clothes, earnestly playing a piano duet.

"Better cross that layout off your list," he advised the leader of the gang when he returned. "They can't have much dough. I seen two people in there playing on one piano!"

———◆———

"In time of trial," pontificated the dominie, "what is our greatest hope?"

The chap on parole, sitting in a rear pew, shouted out the answer. "Acquittal."

In Syracuse there was a fellow who wouldn't worry about acquittal. In fact, he would give the court no cooperation at all. "Guilty or not guilty?" He frowned at the judge. "Figger it out for yourself. That's what you're gettin' paid for."

———◆———

Last summer, hoping to inspire his workers with promptness and energy, a New York executive hung a number of signs reading DO IT NOW around his factory and office.

When he was asked some weeks later how his staff had reacted, he shook his head sadly. "I don't like even to talk about it," he said. "The cashier skipped with $4,000."

———◆———

We'll always have a place in the Hall of Fame, Congress of American Humorists, for Oliver Herford. No story better illustrates his droll humor than the occasion when Herford was the guest of a publishers' association at a sumptuous resort hotel.

Delighted with the lavish treatment, Oliver decided to remain there a few days after the other guests went home. As he was about to leave, he was shocked to learn from the desk clerk that he was expected to pay the balance of the bill himself.

"I haven't that much money with me," he told the clerk.

"That's all right, Mr. Herford. Just give us a check."

"But I haven't any checks, either."

A blank check was supplied and Oliver filled it out.

"I'm sorry, Mr. Herford," said the clerk, "but you've neglected to fill in the name of the bank."

"Ah, yes," said Oliver. "Perhaps you can tell me the name of a good bank."

* * *

Two brothers in the retail coal business had an intricate problem.

"It's a fine thing for you to attend church," said one brother to the other, "but if I get religion, too, who'll weigh the coal?"

While it used to be an old vaudeville plot—the idea of cheating cheaters—we like the version of I. Cahn as told to Walter Winchell.

The burglar had stripped the private museum of all its treasured possessions—precious stones, rare manuscripts, rings, and gems that had once belonged to kings. He picked up the loot-filled bag and was about to exit, when his eyes were attracted to a famous painting on the wall.

He studied the portrait with reverence. He could understand its greatness, because at one time he, too, had had ambitions to paint. So engrossed was he in his study of the picture he hadn't heard the steps behind him until the man spoke.

"Beautiful piece of work, isn't it?" asked the stranger, as the startled felon turned guiltily to face the speaker.

"I'm the curator of the museum," continued the man softly. "I occasionally like to come down here after closing hours and study these paintings alone. Just as you were doing. They always inspire me with their greatness. They're my pride and joy." He pointed to another painting. "This one is a part of the Stuart Collection, a favorite with visitors. And this one here . . ."

He took the art-loving burglar around, showing him various masterpieces. "I could have you locked up for robbing the museum of its priceless treasures," he finally remarked, "but your interest in these works shows that you're not an ordinary thief, that you're inherently gifted with an appreciation of fine things. I'm going to give you a chance to reform."

After the burglar departed silently and gratefully, the other gent stood quietly, studying a Leonardo da Vinci painting, profound admiration written on his face. Then, with a sigh, he picked up the loot-filled bag, cautiously opened the door and—with a furtive look up and down the avenue—slung the bag over his shoulder and hurriedly vanished down the street!

———

The lawyer looked seriously at his client. "As long as you insist on your innocence, I'll gladly defend you with all my zeal and enthusiasm. But are you sure you have told me the entire story?"

The fellow gulped. "Exceptin' where I hid the money."

———

A merchant in Dallas, Texas, asked police to help him decipher the signature on a worthless check. The police did. It was, "U. R. Stuck."

———

The resourcefulness of the police is equaled only by the madcap behavior of our citizens. Recently a man in New York, trying to pick the pocket of a fat man asleep in a subway station, got his hand caught firmly when the sleeper shifted. He was finally extricated by two cops.

When police in Austin, Texas, asked a woman, whose house had been robbed, if she knew who had done the job, they got a straight answer. "Sure, but I want you to find out."

In Pasadena, California, patrolman D. B. Gleason flagged down a motorist who was weaving erratically back and forth across the highway, but let him go when the motorist explained: "Everything's O. K. Just shaving."

---

The yegg removed his shoes and socks. Then his practiced toe began twirling the dials of the safe.

His pal was impatient. "Come on, let's crack this crib and get away from here. Why fool around?"

"Where's your sense of humor?" asked his pal. "This method takes only a few minutes longer and it drives those fingerprint experts nuts."

*"Where's your sense of humor? This method only takes a few minutes longer and it drives those fingerprint experts nuts."*

In Howell, Michigan, the burglars who broke into the American Legion clubhouse set a two-gallon crock of pig hocks on the barroom floor, then rifled the place while the watchdog feasted.

———•–•———

Anita Callahan tells about the army bride looking over the wedding presents from her husband's buddies.

"It's nice to receive such personal gifts as these towels with HIS and HERS embroidered on them. But here is something so intimate and sentimental"—she pointed to an olive drab blanket with the letters US stenciled in the center.

———•–•———

Paul Feinman, a salesman, bought two burglar alarms for his home. Before he had time to install them, they were stolen from his parked automobile.

———•–•———

A certain mad logic is discernible in two recent news stories. A man in Montgomery, Alabama, who was kept awake by his neighbors' dogs, was fined $10 for sitting on his porch at night, howling back.

In Pittsburgh, when police nabbed Clara Habig, they found that her knitting bag, crammed with jewelry, also contained a neatly typewritten Christmas shoplifting list.

———•–•———

The helpful friend offered advice to the fugitive.

"An alibi would help you. Anyone see you at the hour this fellow was shot?"

The fugitive shook his head. "Fortunately, no."

———•–•———

As early as Charles Dickens' *The Pickwick Papers,* the word alibi appears. "Oh, Sammy, Sammy, vy vorn't there a alleybi?"

The misuse of the word always annoyed the late verbal precisionist, Alexander Woollcott. Listen.

"Let me suggest that any man's vocabulary is a more precise and effective means of communication if he carefully reserves the word 'alibi' for its primal eldest meaning, instead of slipping into the sloppy practice of using it as another word for excuse. 'Alibi' is the Latin word for elsewhere and it was the lawyer chaps who first appropriated it for our convenience. If you can prove that when your Aunt Matilda's throat was being slit in Kenosha you yourself— though naturally under suspicion—were engrossed at the time in a game of six-pack bezique in Omaha, you will thereby establish an alibi. It is a handy term and all the color is washed out of it by those who use it for any form of self-exculpation, from a cold in one's head to an unfaithful alarm clock. In America this injurious practice has become so common that to rush now to the defense of the battered old word is probably enlistment in a lost cause."

But it remained for a boy in Harlem to explain it very simply to any interested lexicographer.

"An alibi," he said, "is when you prove you wuz at a prayer meeting where you wasn't to show that you wasn't in somebody's cash register where you wuz."

———•———

"My client only stole a few dollars to ease his hunger," pleaded the lawyer for another who had dallied with the law. "The proof? Nearby was a pocketbook with $200 in it. Untouched."

The lawyer turned around. His client was sobbing. "Does my plea have that effect on you?"

"I'm crying," said his client, "because this is the first knowledge I've had of that $200."

———•———

On the other hand, there are certain intrepid souls who willingly waltz into the calaboose. Here are Exhibits A and B.

"Will all you crap-shooters please come forward?" said Judge Walter L. Kimmel in calling a gambling case in Tulsa, Oklahoma.

Six men walked to the bench. Only five men had been charged.

"What are you doing here?" the judge asked the other.

"I can shoot craps," said the man.

In Minneapolis, a man who was tapped on the shoulder by a policeman during a roundup of drunks got into the patrol wagon and went to jail. In court he learned that the cop had just wanted to ask him to move out of the way.

---

In our daily lives we have an assortment of minor crimes that validate a statement made by C. A. Helvetius back in 1758, "There is not a crime but is placed among honest actions by the one to whom the crime is advantageous."

As listed by W. E. Farbstein, there was the Chicago motorist who drove for years without a license. He couldn't have obtained a license had he sought one. He was getting a state pension for blindness.

A woman in Buffalo was arrested for shoplifting. She said she had tried a hat on that was so tiny she was not aware it was on her head when she walked out.

A Santa Clara motorist gave as his excuse for speeding that he must have been pushed along by a heavy tail wind.

A Chicago youth, failing to report for army duty, said the notification didn't state what year.

---

Attorney Harold Bogin tells the one about the police judge in a booming western mining town who solved a legal perplexity in his own way. He leered at the pickpocket. "I fine you fifteen dollars."

"Your honor, I simply can't pay it. I haven't but ten dollars with me."

The judge then announced to the crowd of spectators: "The court will now take a recess of five minutes while the defendant circulates among those present. He will then report to me."

———•••———

Fulton Oursler, always an entertaining yarn spinner, gives us another slant on western justice.

The FBI agent in a western state was hot on the trail of a fugitive. When word came that he was heading for a small town, the G-man called the local sheriff.

"You send me a pitcher of that guy and I'll git him good," the sheriff promised.

That night the government agent mailed the sheriff not one but a dozen pictures of the wanted man—profile, full face, standing, sitting, and in various costumes.

Within twenty-four hours he received an electrifying telephone call: "We got eleven of them crooks locked up already," the sheriff boasted, "and I guarantee to jug the last one before morning."

———•———

Mordecai Dancis comes up with some of the funniest yarns you've heard. For instance:

During World War II, screaming police sirens whistled along Washington's streets. Eight motorcycles, jammed with officers and Secret Service operatives, preceded a long, black limousine that drew up to the White House.

Two boys watched the cavalcade. "Look," said the older, "do you know who those men are? With all those policemen? That's President Roosevelt and Winston Churchill."

"Yeah?" said the younger boy. "What have they done?"

———•••———

Counsellor Bernard Grossman's subtle wit is the source of this one:

Hearing a strange noise in the night, the Quaker investigated and found a burglar ransacking the kitchen. He took his fowling piece and called down from the stair landing, "Friend, I would do thee no harm for all the world—but thee standest where I am about to shoot."

— • —

In the tough, hardy days of the rollicking and robust west, the college man from the east inherited a cattle ranch. Discovering his neighbor was engaged in a slight case of rustling, the college man wrote the appropriate note:

"I would be grateful if you won't leave your hot branding irons where my cattle can sit down on them."

— • —

Here are a few choice items revealing the selectivity exercised by our artists in grand larceny.

Near Steubenville, Ohio, thieves stole a mile of railroad track from a Pennsylvania Railroad spur.

H. A. Fitzgerald constructed a 158-apartment building in Chicago. While it was still unfinished, thieves entered and stole 158 tubs.

In Miami, the Homestead Machinery Company reported the theft of a 10-ton steamroller.

In Little Falls, New York, James Hallinan reported the theft of a granite monument weighing 1,600 pounds.

Posing as repairmen, two burglars entered the basement of Joseph T. Cousins in Kansas City, dismantled the heating plant, and removed it by truck.

— • —

Irving Bacheller gives us an insight into Kentucky gentility.

A planter discovered a poor neighbor in the act of stealing a ham from his smokehouse. "Joe, I'm glad you came for that ham. I was going to send it over to your house today."

— • —

In the neighboring state of Tennessee, high in the hills, a mountaineer approached the owner of the still.

"Wan' some corn likker."

The purveyor of the potables had a question to ask.

"Got two kinds of corn likker to sell. Yer kin have what yer feelin's call fer—courtin' likker or fightin' likker?"

*"Got two kinds of corn likker to sell. Yer kin have what yer feelin's call fer—courtin' likker or fightin' likker?"*

Only your local lawyers and your police department aren't amazed by the odd occurrences every day in any part of our country.

Not long ago, the police of San Pedro, California, arrested Jesus Diaz, who had smashed into three police cars, caromed off into a fourth, and come to a stop in front of the police station.

Perhaps it's the California air. A man in San Juan Bautista aimlessly fired a .45 pistol near the Casa Maria social hall. He learned too late, after his speedy arrest, that a score of policemen were having a banquet there.

Then there was the young couple in Hoboken, New Jersey, who succeeded in stealing a watch, but failed in their quick getaway by hailing a police car they mistook for a taxi.

———•———

"What is this, a stick-up?" asked the priest, as he opened the rectory door to be confronted by a revolver aimed directly at him.

"No, Father," said the young man. "I've just been appointed to the police force and I want you to bless the gun."

———•———

Further proof that a policeman's lot is not a happy one is furnished by two cases recently reported by the press.

Albert D. Martin of Sterling, Illinois, sued two policemen for $10,000. He complained that if they had arrested him for drunken driving five minutes sooner he would never have had a smashup.

The second case concerns a policeman in River Edge, New Jersey. When he wrote the Rev. Walter J. Poynton a ticket he was forced to admit that he didn't have his own license with him and meekly accepted a ticket himself when the parson called another cop.

———•———

In Zanesville, Ohio, a woman complained to police that a thief had not only stolen milk from her doorstep but had left orders for whipping cream.

———•———

A candidate for the police force in Cincinnati lost his chance for a job because he was too honest.

He told interviewing officials he "didn't care much about

being on the force, but the graft ought to be good downtown because of all the saloons."

Patrolman John H. Davis of Seattle was assigned to the waterfront to round up sleeping vagrants on the docks. He was eventually rounded up himself and suspended for thirty days, for sleeping on the docks while on duty.

---

A storekeeper of Ripley, New York, advertised the combination of his safe in a local paper.

The safe had been carried away by thieves who left a polite note saying, that if they found the combination in the classified advertisements, they would *not* use nitroglycerin on it. They were sorry, but you know how it is. Times are tough.

A few days later the safe was returned to the storekeeper, empty but undamaged.

---

"Hey, don't make so much noise," said John Cronin to a burglar who broke into his house in Watertown, Massachusetts. "I've got sinus trouble."

"Well," said the burglar, "what you need is a good massage. Look . . ." and with that he rolled up his sleeves and massaged Cronin's head. Mr. Cronin felt so much better that he told the burglar where to find a few dollars.

---

When the police told George Neumann that the thief who had taken his traveling bag from his car would probably keep the contents and discard the bag, Neumann got an idea. He advertised in a newspaper asking the thief to throw the bag into the yard of a friend. The bag turned up at the specified place.

---

John Deering, a truck driver of Anderson, Indiana, was stranded along the road with a burned-out fuse. Two men drove alongside and relieved him of fifteen dollars—but supplied him with a fuse before they fled.

In St. Joseph, Missouri, when a seventeen-year-old customer returned to the Townsend and Wall department store to complain that a costly cigarette lighter he had bought was no good, the store manager retorted that neither was his check for $124.22.

A party motoring through Idaho came upon a lonely sheepherder high up in the mountains, and asked him what he did to amuse himself.

"Oh, I hold up motorists and rob 'em," replied the sheepherder.

"But aren't you likely to be arrested and sent to jail?"

"Nope. I do it this way. Ye see this hairpin bend in the road? Well, I hold up the people right here, and then when they go on I duck over the hill, take off my mask, put on my badge, and meet 'em down at the bend. 'I jist caught that fella that robbed ye,' I sez. 'Here's yer valuables.' There's no danger in it, and it's kinda excitin'."

———•—•———

Ashtrays in the judges' library of the U.S. Circuit Court of Appeals in New York are labeled: "Not government property. Please do not take from library."

———•—•———

Two strangers in a first-class compartment were in friendly conversation. The windows had been closed by previous occupants, and the talk had drifted to the subject of ventilation. "I make it," said one, "an invariable practice to advise people to sleep with their bedroom windows open all year round."

"Ho, ho!" laughed the other. "It is easy to see your profession."

"Indeed, and what do you think it is?"

"It is fairly obvious that you're a doctor."

"Not at all," retorted the first, very confidentially. "To tell you the truth, I'm a—burglar!"

———•———

There are other twists to the crime problem.

"Can you do double entry?" asked the employer of the prospective employee.

"I can do triple entry!" was the reply.

"Triple entry?"

"Yes—one entry for the working partner showing the true profits; another for the sleeping partner showing small profits, and a third for the income tax collector showing a loss."

And Will Weiss, who gave up the violin for law, knows a big bankruptcy lawyer who left the courtroom to call his office to find out if anybody wanted to fail. When he came back, a friend asked him the news. He replied, "No, no one wants to fail—but a client wanted to know if he should have a fire."

———•———

Pocket-picking is a recognized profession highly unionized in Egypt. When King Farouk was married, the King of the Thieves issued a proclamation in the newspapers, in which he promised, as a friendly gesture to the other king, to call off all his thieves during the nuptial celebrations. And not a pocket was picked.

———•———

Here is an advertisement that appeared in the Atlanta *Constitution*.

Want to hide? Vanish temporarily or permanently, so no male or female gyps, mean in-laws, grafters, gold-diggers, ex-love blackmailers, or other pests can find you? I can hide you so, and protect you, in my Georgia pine forest sanctuary. My price is $60, winter season; $90 yearly. Address your problem in confidence. Chief White Cougar, Jessup, Ga.

The elementary facts of life were supplied to a judge in Dayton, Ohio, by a confidence man.

"How could you swindle people who trusted you?"

"Judge, you can't swindle people who don't trust you."

———•—•———

Because her lawyer husband continually preached about the wisdom of making each household servant present references, Mrs. Bigelow asked the applicant, "Where are your references?"

"I hate to show 'em, ma'am. Like my photographs, they don't do me justice."

———•—•———

The police had been after him for years, but never could pin the evidence on him. One night they brought him in for questioning.

Young McNamara, one of the new school of detectives, who thinks persuasion is better than a fist in the face, opened up with praise of the culprit's prowess.

"Spike, I don't know how you do it. But it's masterful."

Ten minutes more of such blandishments ensued before Spike opened his trap. They all pressed forward to hear his confession. But all that Spike did was to smile and say, "Flattery will get you nowhere."

———•—•———

Life started from a cell and if justice prevails a good many people should end there. But many of them get away. Take Jerry Mitchell's story.

The case hadn't been going so well, and the judge was beginning to feel sorry for the young lawyer, who was defending his first criminal case. His client stood to get a very severe sentence if the trial continued.

"Counsellor," he told him, "I have no objection to calling a recess to give you an opportunity to give your client the best advice you can think of."

The recess was taken and, when it was over, the young lawyer returned but his client was not in court.

"Where's the defendant?" asked the judge.

"He's skipped, your honor," replied the lawyer. "He took my advice, the best advice I could think of."

Joe Bash, Mercer County counsel, tells a similar story that happened in New Jersey. Two friends met.

"I've got to sail for Europe immediately," said the first.

"Why let a doctor scare you? You look healthy to me," replied the other.

"This is not a doctor's advice. It's my lawyer's."

———•—•———

America should soon realize that Ollie Crawford, whose column *Headline Hopping* appears every morning in the Philadelphia *Inquirer,* is one of the country's greatest wits. Let us illustrate.

Ollie read a headline in his own paper that Philadelphia gamblers had, through devious techniques and stratagems, been able to select the judge who would sentence them upon conviction. Here is his chronicle.

Gamblers picked own judges for trials, grand jury finds. A gambler, it seems, is a guy who doesn't take chances.

He likes odds, but not the judge who'll give him 10 to 20.

These boys were in favor of more safety in numbers. They didn't mind writing numbers, but they didn't want to wear them. For guys who handled a lot of slips, they didn't make many. They may have been tinhorn gamblers, but they knew when to blow.

A gambler is a guy who makes his bet and has to lie out of it.

The jury said the boys wouldn't pick a bench until they found out who was riding it. They figured the judge on the basis of what he did the last time out. The lighter the sentence the heavier the play. Some of the boys spent less time in prison than the guy who delivers the milk. When they went to Moyamensing, they used the revolving door.

In this system, a guy could go to jail after the first race and be out for the daily double. If his horses were that fast, he'd have retired long ago.

The system worked fine for all but one gambler. He had two raps against him and tried to parlay them.

* * *

Thieves who broke into Barbara Kloberdan's Denver apartment, took $30 cash, $49 worth of clothes, ate some potato salad, and drank some Scotch. Then, finding varnish and a brush in the kitchen cabinet, they touched up the door they had splintered to get in.

* * *

The legitimate swag, if such there be, is taken from the nightclub habitues, who pay disproportionate prices to be seen by people they care less than nothing for.

George Riley, in *Furlough Fun* over NBC, states the case: "I like the atmosphere in this nightclub. Some clubs take you to Havana, some take you to Algiers. This club just takes you."

* * *

Occasionally, as W. S. Gilbert points out, there's punishment to fit the crime.

Judge Richard Hughes looked down on the student defendant. "Young man, you are charged with taking hundreds of pieces of silverware from a fraternity house. For your sentence I am hereby making you return every piece of that silverware to the hotels it was originally taken from."

* * *

Here are more quaint characters who keep the police from relaxing.

In Philadelphia a stranger who stopped to help Walter Bowe push his stalled car, suggested that he work the starter while Bowe pushed. He then managed to start the motor and disappeared with the car.

Police in Portland not long ago received the following note: "The guy who lives next to the police station is a crook and ought to be prosecuted to the fullest extent of the law. I cracked his safe last night and found nothing but counterfeit money. Signed, A Friend."

In New Orleans a burglar stole Patrolman Joseph Bowman's pants, badge, cartridge belt, and $13.50 from his house on Piety Street. Bowman explained to Capt. Edward Delatte that he had returned home tired out from guarding other people's property and had gone to sleep. He was so tired, he said, that he didn't even turn over when the burglar opened a kitchen window and stole the pants and cartridge belt from a doorknob. The badge and money were in the pants pockets.

"How could I seize him?" said a rookie patrolman to a superior officer in Long Beach. "Why, Sarge, I had my gun in one hand and my club in the other."

---

Yeah, maybe these lads on the fringe of society get fun out of their work. Take the kidnaping job in St. Paul.

"Shall we hold this cutie for ransom, Boss?" asked Davey the Drip.

The boss sneered. "Let Ransom get his own wimmen."

---

Does crime pay?

In this chapter we've skirted the answer. Fact is, we can't tell you just yet. We're in the same position as a dramatist reported by Albert R. Perkins.

The dramatist, employed to write stories from the Bible in radio form, was astonished, at the end of a broadcast, to hear the announcer say:

"Will Cain kill Abel? Tune in at the same time tomorrow morning and find out."

# CHAPTER 9

# Pen Pals

IT REQUIRED the imprimatur of Oscar Wilde (*The Ballad of Reading Gaol*) to teach mankind to stay out of prison. But you couldn't prove it with Elmer Howard, of Harlan, Kentucky. He was arrested for breaking into the local hoosegow.

Not all malefactors share Elmer's enthusiasm for the familiar life. One "con" looked petulantly at the social worker who was imparting her philosophy. "Remember, my good man," she said, "as Richard Lovelace wrote, 'Stone walls do not a prison make, nor iron bars a cage.'"

"You mean that, lady? Then I'm nuts to be stayin' here these past five years."

But there was a toper taken off to Sing Sing who said he didn't mind going there. "There are bars all over the place."

Whether or not crime pays, it keeps the D.A. and the defense counsel busy every moment. More juries seem to be "hung" than murderers. But that's our cautious American system of jurisprudence. We don't "commit" the murderer until we're sure beyond a reasonable doubt that he committed the murder.

Another actor in this daily crime tableau is the judge. He sits there on Olympus fully aware that the law is whatever is boldly asserted and plausibly maintained. And when the trial is over he receives condemnation from both sides for his fair and impartial handling of the case. But that's life.

Take Jake. He, too, could write a sonnet on the vagaries of crime.

Jake's mob had reached its hiding place after blowing up the First National Bank vaults. One of the boys had not returned. It was Benny the Booper. He was now on a cold slab at the morgue, his body tattooed with lead.

"Boys," began the Big Guy, "we're sure gonna miss Benny. Now, I ain't one for deliverin' an allergy over a pal. I don't have the woids. But dis I'll say. Benny was one of de best rods in de business. Ever since he broke out of reform school he knew how to operate. After me, he was Public Enemy Number Two."

Jake curled his lip. He whispered to another member of the mob. "Ain't dis a lousy racket? Yer gotta get bumped off before anyone says a few kind woids about yer."

---

In another chapter most of the case histories pertain to the Artful Dodgers (applause from the audience, even though we are not referring to the Brooklyn baseball team). This section concerns itself with those who didn't get away. Mike offers a good example.

He met Joe, who was being escorted to the State Penitentiary by two officers. Mike said to his wife, Mabel, "There's my old pal, Joe. Wait'll I say hello."

Mike stepped forward. "What's the situation, Joe? Why have these cops got you?"

"I killed my wife, Mike. My trial just ended. They're taking me to State Prison for six weeks—"

Mike interrupted. "Six weeks for shooting your wife? Mabel, turn around. I want to give you something I've been thinking about for years." He thereupon drew his gun and killed Mabel.

"Yes," continued Joe, "six weeks in State Prison. Then I go to the chair."

Maybe a cartoon by George Wolfe explains one cause of juvenile delinquency. The man with the badge has just seated himself in his own kitchen while his wife is putting lunch on the table. There stands Junior bawling out his pater in these words, "How can I ever live it down? My own father a truant officer!"

A truant officer, let it be understood, is merely a talent scout for the reform school.

A script submitted for the radio program, "Junior G-men," in which a band of tots solved crimes which baffled their elders, was okayed except for the phrase "He has a heart of stone."

"You can't expect a child to know what that means," the program director said. He thought for a minute and then said, "Change it to 'He's a yellow rat.'"

A visitor to another children's radio program saw a ripe cantaloupe completely squashed on the sound-effects table.

"What was the cantaloupe used for?" he asked.

The sound man told him, "That's the only way we can convince the kids that someone's head is being bashed in with a hammer."

A lawyer in Chicago worried about the crime potential of his son.

Little Paul, aged six, was addicted to the use of profane language, a source of much grief to his parents. Naturally they were loath to have him appear in company where his loquaciousness was the cause of much embarrassment to them.

He was invited to a birthday party in the neighborhood and, after much persuasion accompanied by promises not to say any bad words, he prevailed on his parents to let him go. Dressed up like a cherub and bearing his gift, he set out for the party. In half an hour or less he was back, still carrying his gift.

His mother, assuming she knew the cause, without a word undressed him, thrashed him soundly, and put him to bed. When his father came home, he was told what had happened and went upstairs with fire in his eyes. As he opened the door, little Paul threw up both hands and said:

"Just a minute, Dad. The damned party isn't till tomorrow!"

———•———

Dr. H. A. Clegg in *Brush Up Your Health* explains that civilized man turns his homicidal feelings into repressions. That is, some of us do.

Says Dr. Clegg, "You are, of course, an over-inhibited and repressed savage. It is really only a short time ago that you were pursuing your next cave neighbor with the laudable intention of cracking his head; and there was still the evening meal to kill in order to celebrate the event . . . An emotion well under way needs for its satisfaction expression in muscular activity. Anger should be logically (and psychologically) ended in a well-planted blow. Hate needs a little homicide to keep it quiet. Is not the golf ball a convenient symbol for the head of the man who did you such a dirty deal last week?"

One such civilized man vented his anger by firing his gun.

His lawyer pleaded for leniency. "After all, Judge, he didn't aim it at anyone. Just fired in the air."

The judge wasn't moved. "That'll be $25 and costs. He might have hit an angel."

———•———

Edward Streeter, who gave us that delightful hymn to Hymen, *Father of the Bride,* discussed a campaign once launched by *Redbook* magazine.

A committee appointed by the magazine to study the question of how best to hold a wife, wrote to a selected list of husbands.

The only reply received was from a certain western penitentiary. It stated briefly: "I found the best way was around the neck, but it should not be overdone. Please note change of address."

* * *

Every day the D.A. has to prosecute the oddest cases. This happened in New York.

"What's the charge?" The judge looked at the prisoner.

"Kidnaping," said the D.A.

"That's a lie, Judge. I'm just an overcoat thief."

"What do you say to that, Mr. D.A.?"

"He's telling the truth, Judge, but this time he forgot to take the man out of the overcoat."

* * *

In another of his incomparable harlequinades, Peter Arno has a *New Yorker* cartoon showing two men entering a Pullman diner.

Handcuffs hold one to the other and it is obvious that here is another errant soul wafting his way to Sing Sing.

The obsequious steward is inquiring diplomatically, "Together?"

* * *

Dr. George Kirchway was once talking to a group of young lawyers. "I was dean of Columbia Law School before I became warden of Sing Sing.

"I meet many men on the street today," he continued, "whose faces are familiar but whose names I have forgotten. I never know whether to say, 'When did you graduate?' or 'When did you get out?'"

* * *

What the lawyers would call *"Nolo contendere"* and laymen "Punishment to fit the crime" is portrayed in one of the most delightful books about lawyers, the autobiography of John C. Knox, *A Judge Comes of Age* (Charles Scribner's Sons, New York). One of the most interesting stories concerns the cross-examination of a "rotund, cherubic, soft-voiced and lisping" Negro who was testifying against his former companions in a mass bootlegging trial. After a series of vilifying and browbeating questions directed at this witness by one of the defense counsel, each of which boomeranged, "the attorney," recounts Judge Knox, "certain now that he had as yet failed to create the impression before the jury for which he had hoped, decided to make one more effort. It seemed to me that I saw certain signs of desperation. The lawyer pointed dramatically at the Negro.

" 'For what else have you been arrested?' he demanded.

" 'Well, suh,' came the soft reply, 'theah's nuthin' Ah kin recollect.'

" 'Do you mean that?' shouted the lawyer.

" 'Yes, suh. Ah means whateveh Ah says, suh.'

"With a solemn manner and a deep voice the lawyer offered another question.

" 'Do you mean to tell this court and jury that you were not arrested for rape?'

" 'Oh, yes, suh,' he smiled. 'Ah clean forgot 'bout dat. It jes' slipped mah mind.'

" 'And what did you get for that?' shrieked the lawyer.

"I listened intently for the answer, and so, I am sure, did every juror. Yet the Negro's manner did not change an iota, and his voice, if anything, grew still softer.

" 'Married,' he replied."

---

In Lewiston, Maine, Judge Adrien Cote refused to send "Bosco" Boulet to the county jail because the last time he had kicked about the food too much.

---

In San Francisco, after Frank Avilez, Jr., was convicted of assault, he appealed his 400-year prison sentence and got sixty years knocked off.

The Virginia judge, a great rhetorician, looked cheerfully at the man about to be sentenced.

"On next Wednesday morning, at the bright and early hour of five, the mockingbird will be exercising its imitative tonsils beneath the pungent branches of the persimmon tree . . .

"The bluebirds will be humming dulcet tunes to a thousand mates in nearby trees, and the warm Virginia breezes will, like so many gentle zephyrs, kiss the sycamore and the pine . . .

"The sap will be coursing gayly through the pulsating cottonwood . . . all Nature, in the ecstasy of its joyous, seasonal exuberance, will call out carols of lyric beauty . . . but you, you bastard, will enjoy none of it . . . because I hereby sentence you to die at midnight Tuesday."

———•———

Only a convict likes to be stopped in the middle of a sentence. But we have death house records to show that some of the lads hate to wait for a certain period. That's the date when the state wants to close the books against them. Such as the chap about to be hanged. According to John Kieran, the fellow was asked if he had anything to say.

"Yes, I sure do. I want to say this is going to be a lesson to me."

Another one of the departees turned to Warden Spencer Miller and said, "You'll take care of the electric bill, won't you, Warden?"

While Sir Walter Raleigh was imprisoned in the Tower of London the barber came to dress his beard. But Raleigh refused, saying, "At present, friend, there is a lawsuit pending between me and the king about this head, and I don't intend to lay out any money upon it until it is decided which of us it is to belong to."

The warden informed one of the boys in Alabama, "It's

ON NEXT WEDNESDAY MORNING, AT THE BRIGHT AND EARLY HOUR OF FIVE, THE MOCKINGBIRD WILL BE EXERCISING ITS IMITATIVE TONSILS BENEATH THE PUNGENT BRANCHES OF THE PERSIMMON TREE . . .

THE BLUEBIRDS WILL BE HUMMING DULCET TUNES TO A THOUSAND MATES IN NEARBY TREES, AND THE WARM VIRGINIA BREEZES WILL, LIKE SO MANY GENTLE ZEPHYRS, KISS THE SYCAMORE AND THE PINE . . .

THE SAP WILL BE COURSING GAYLY THROUGH THE PULSATING COTTONWOOD . . . ALL NATURE, IN THE ECSTASY OF ITS JOYOUS, SEASONAL EXUBERANCE, WILL CALL OUT CAROLS OF LYRIC BEAUTY . . . BUT YOU, YOU BASTARD, WILL ENJOY NONE OF IT . . . BECAUSE I HEREBY SENTENCE YOU TO DIE AT MIDNIGHT TUESDAY.

your last meal. You can have anything you want."

"Thanks," he said. "I'll take watermelon."

"But this is December," pleaded the warden. "Water-melons aren't planted yet, much less ripe."

The other smiled. "I can wait."

---

The defendant had a long-winded lawyer who orated for hours. He sent a note to the judge.

"If I should be found guilty, would the court please credit my sentence with all the unnecessary time taken up by my lawyer?"

---

Chris Schlaich contributes this one:

A floorwalker, tired of his job, gave it up and joined the police force. Several months later a friend asked him how he liked being a policeman.

"Well," he replied, "the pay and the hours are good, but what I like best of all is that the customer is always wrong."

---

One customer who was "dead" wrong lay on the icy slab of the morgue.

The detective from the homicide squad ended his report on a cryptic note. "There were powder marks on his body before and after she shot him."

---

Lawyers are always afraid of the ad lib statement, even from their own witnesses. An attorney in Wichita swooned when he heard one of his character witnesses in a murder trial.

"What's Bill's reputation? I'd say he's always been a straight shooter."

---

In California a kind-hearted and simple-minded old prune grower was elected county judge, practically without oppo-sition. Almost the first case he had in his official capacity

"There were powder marks on his body before and after she shot him."

was a Mexican youth who, in a fit of pique growing out of a domestic difference, took an ax and chopped his aged parents into small fragments. The brutality of the crime aroused the whole countryside, and when the man was captured and arraigned before the new county judge for a preliminary hearing, the courtroom was crowded with citizens.

The prisoner maintained a rather bored and indifferent silence. Witnesses testified to the finding of the dismembered bodies, and the prosecutor then demanded that the murderer be remanded to jail to await the action of the grand jury.

Before authorizing this step, his honor plainly felt it incumbent to say something appropriate to the circumstances.

Gazing over his spectacles at the stolid youth, he clucked reprovingly with his tongue several times, and then delivered himself of this utterance:

"Now, looka here, son! You know you ain't been actin' right!"

———•———

Such understatement equals the Peter Arno cartoon of the wife, at a bridge foursome, shooting her husband.

The other husband looks impassively at his wife and says, "Well, I guess that breaks up our little game."

———•———

"The defendant is so crooked," began the D.A. in his opening to the jury, "that when he gets up in the morning, he has to screw his socks on. He lived in one home for twenty years. He'd be there yet if the governor hadn't pardoned him."

———•———

Another character with taking ways was Carlos dos Santos of Rio de Janeiro, who was arrested during a routine round-up of pickpockets. He was about to be released when the station detective rearrested him because he discovered that his wallet had been pinched during the questioning.

"Thus conscience does make cowards of us all," said Hamlet.

Want proof?

The title of "King of Quacks" was claimed in a recent BBC broadcast on behalf of a certain long-dead Italian named Mantacinnie, who made a huge sum by undertaking to revive the dead.

Mantacinnie claimed to have discovered the elixir of life, and said that to prove it he would raise all the people of Lyons, France, who had recently died.

In due course, Mantacinnie announced the great day when he would revive the dead. "We shall be up all night," he said to his partner. "We shall have a lot of callers."

It happened just as he said: there was a stream of muffled figures seeking private interviews, and a clinking underneath their cloaks suggested bags of money.

"My father died a year ago," said the first. "He was a rich miser, and it will go hard with me tomorrow when he sees how much I have spent. Here is one thousand guineas to leave him out."

The next one was a beautiful young woman in great distress. "I'll give you anything not to bring back the tyrant who was my husband," she sobbed. "Last week I married my beloved Jacques, and we cannot be parted again so soon."

Some of Mantacinnie's callers feared that the dear departed might be curious as to the sudden "illnesses" that had carried them away.

But better was to come. The mayor and town council appeared, in full regalia, and begged an audience. "Learned sir," said the mayor, "I must beg of you to have pity on us. The resurrection of our predecessors in office would throw the present holders into poverty and the whole city into confusion; accept this small tribute to your powers, and go and leave us in peace."

But Mantacinnie was not yet contented. "That's all very well," he said, "but people will doubt the truth of my power to raise your dead."

"That can easily be arranged," replied the mayor. "I will give you a solemn document testifying that we ourselves have witnessed your wonderful powers."

———•—•———

The ingenuity of the boys already behind the bars worries the turnkeys.

In San Quentin, California, George Vierra, serving a seven-year stretch, got a sentence of one to six more years after guards found him in his cell preparing marijuana that he got from the prison stone quarry.

And a warden in Pittsburgh had to post this notice in the dining room bulletin board:

> SOMEONE BURGLED MY SAFE LAST NIGHT.
> IF I CATCH THE CONVICT WHO DID IT . . .
> OUT HE GOES.

———•—•———

While George Page was warden of the New Jersey State Penitentiary, he had the friendly habit of stopping and talking to the inmates.

One morning he spoke to a lad who seemed out of place in this Cathedral de Coop. "What are you in for, boy?"

"Borrowing money."

"That doesn't sound like a felony," said George.

"Oh, I had to knock the man down three or four times before he agreed to lend me the money."

There was another day when a church social worker interviewed the warden.

"Does drink bring most of these prisoners here?" she asked.

"Lady," said Warden Page, "I'm the only one who can get a drink in this place."

The editors of Utah's state prison newspaper had a consoling word for their fellow convicts: "No one is entirely useless. Even the worst of us can serve as horrible examples."

A prison trusty in Jefferson City, Missouri, finished off his weekly sermon at the penitentiary with the text: "I go to prepare a place for you . . . that where I am, there ye may be also." A few hours later he escaped.

---

In Olympia, Washington, they tell about the illiterate prisoner who learned to read and write while in the state reformatory. He was paroled, then bounced back in jail to serve a term for forgery.

---

A visitor at Connecticut State Prison asked a prisoner, "What's your name?"

The prisoner sneered, "9742."

"Is that your real name?"

"Naw," he said, "just me pen name."

---

When "Big Tim" Murphy was warden of the New Jersey State Penitentiary, he was extremely nervous at the first execution he had to supervise.

One of the five men to be electrocuted insisted on speaking. He stood with his hand on the electric chair as he made an earnest espousal of his innocence. The clock ticked on and there were still four men to be dispatched.

After listening for forty-five minutes to the plea of the condemned man, Warden Murphy could take no more. Wiping the perspiration from his own face, he spoke to the other. "Joe, why don't you just sit down and relax?"

---

An Alan Dunn cartoon is set in police headquarters. The third degree lights burn fiercely on the balding brow of the hardened criminal. Present are the police stenographer and the tough detective with a segment of rubber hose in his brawny fist.

But the "con" is in an expansive mood. There is no need for rough stuff. He tells the detectives, "Well, there you are. I guess all I needed was someone to draw me out."

———•———

According to Neal O'Hara, the authorities in one of England's prisons, instead of slapping unruly prisoners into solitary confinement, force them to don pink rayon panties and parade in this feminine garb before their fellow convicts.

———•———

Warden Lawes at Sing Sing once had an execution scheduled for Monday.

When he visited the condemned man to break the news, the man was in a cheerful mood.

"Can't you electrocute me on a Saturday, instead?"

"What's wrong with Monday?" asked the warden.

"Oh," sighed the man, "it seems such a poor way to start the week."

———•———

Mrs. O'Leary, over the back porch, could see unusual preparations in the home of Mrs. O'Tamash. The soda water was stacked up in cases. A barrel of beer was set up in the yard.

"Are you having a party, Mrs. O'Tamash?"

"Yes, Mrs. O'Leary, tonight. A coming out party."

"For your daughter Mary?"

"No, for Timmie and Leo."

"Why, I thought they were in for three years."

"They were. But with good behavior, they're getting out today."

"Ah, Mrs. O'Tamash," said the neighbor, " 'tis a proud mother you must be with two such fine, strapping lads as Timmie and Leo."

Two friends met in Milwaukee. "Where have you been?" asked one.

"I've been away for ten days."

"What doing?"

"Ten days."

# CHAPTER 10

# *When Compensation Sets In*

THE SCANTILY-CLAD LADY was being carried down the ladder by the agile fireman.

"Madam," he said, "you are quite naked."

"Oh, not, I'm not," she argued. "I'm covered by insurance."

Today, in this great land of ours, most of us, whether we need it or not, are covered by insurance of some kind. And despite the fine print, which one jurist excoriated (De Lancey vs. Rockingham Farmers Mutual Fire Insurance Co.: 52, New Hampshire, 581), "Seldom has the art of typography been so successfully diverted from the diffusion of knowledge to the suppression of it as in some insurance policies," the insurance companies endeavor to live up to every phase of the law. It is big business and there is little desire for sharp practice. All the insurance companies have to protect themselves in the clinches. The land is filled with guys and gals, who, in an accident, have enough savvy to close their eyes until a lawyer arrives. In the field of workmen's compensation, the history of most injuries show great improvement the moment "compensation sets in." And as for fire insurance! Ed Wynn stated the case exactly when he asked a clothing store proprietor how business was. "Not so good, Ed. It looks like a sure-fire proposition."

*"You took out a fire insurance policy with our company at eleven this morning. Please explain the delay."*

One fire insurance company, perplexed by a case on its books, dispatched a letter to the policyholder:

"You took out a policy with our company at 11 A.M., August 16th. Your place was gutted by fire at 3 P.M. the same day. Kindly explain the delay."

———◆———

Hollywood director Mervyn LeRoy received a letter from an insurance company containing this line:

"This sum will be paid you in a single sum at the time of your death, which we understand is what you prefer."

———•—•———

Victor Borge, the Danish comic, received a thrashing from his father when Papa came home one night to find Victor standing in the parlor before the roaring fire.

The Borge home didn't have a fireplace.

———•—•———

Frank J. V. Gimino was trying a workmen's compensation case, representing an elderly Italian who had been burned about the legs following an acid explosion in the plant. When the bandages were removed, he was considerably pock-marked.

Testifying for the insurance company as an expert witness was the venerable and beloved Dr. William J. Arlitz.

"Tell me, Doctor," asked Counsellor Gimino, "whether you think these pock-marks constitute a cosmetic defect?"

"Yes," replied Dr. Arlitz. This was a startling admission. It might indicate a higher compensation award. And coming from the insurance company's doctor . . . well, even Gimino was astonished.

"Ah," he said, "then you do think these pock-marks are a cosmetic defect."

"Yes," said Dr. Arlitz, looking at the aged, weather-beaten laborer, "if you are going to make a ballet dancer out of him."

———•—•———

Dr. Bloom, of Trenton, was being cross-examined by Edward Katzenbach in a compensation case.

"What did your examination show, Doctor?"

"I found the sphincter ani muscles were injured."

"And where are these muscles?"

"If I had a chart here," answered Dr. Bloom, "I could show you. But if I stood up I can point them out to you."

"Please do so, Doctor."

Dr. Bloom's index finger pointed to his fundament. "In here," he said.

"Thank you, Doctor," said courteous counsel, "and would you now step toward the court stenographer and have the exhibit marked?"

———•—•———

"Is this the Fidelity Insurance Company?" asked an anxious female voice.

"It is."

"How much do you charge to insure my husband's fidelity?"

———•—•———

It was an important insurance case, but the plaintiff's lawyer was confident because he had spotted a good friend on the jury.

After three days of testimony the case went to the jury. They came in with a disappointing award. The lawyer sought his friend on the jury. "What happened?"

"Oh, the usual disagreement. Six of the jury wanted to give your man $3,500, while six wanted to give him $3,000. I spoke up, 'Let's split the difference,' so that, pal, is how we awarded your client $500."

———•—•———

In Melbourne, Australia, the Underwriters Council approved full benefits under the Workers Compensation Act for anyone who dislocated his jaw while yawning at work.

And whether the gag writers or even Earl Wilson believes it, the New Jersey Disability Benefits Fund paid a claim to a washerwoman who found a protrusive part of her anatomy caught in the wringer.

———•—•———

It had been a successful fire and now the owner of the gutted business was in the lawyer's office receiving his money.

"Why are you taking such a big fee?" asked the client.

"Well, the matter has been in litigation for some time."

The client was not impressed. "You'd think *you* started the fire," he said, as he picked up the money and departed.

* * *

Clancy fell off the scaffolding. There were so many problems with the estate, so many conferences in the insurance company office that when Mrs. Clancy returned home, thorougly fatigued, she confided to her children, "There's so much trouble that sometimes I wish your father hadn't fallen off the building."

* * *

Ben Krupkin tells a similar tale of little Valentine Shapiro who wanted to swim in the deeper waters at Coney Island.

"You stay near Mama, Valentine."

"But look at Papa. He's away out."

"That's different, Valentine. Papa's insured."

* * *

There was a truthful insurance agent in Vincennes, Indiana. A man edged up to him, asking, "If I took out insurance on my wife today and tomorrow she died, what would I get?"

The agent told him. "The chair."

* * *

She had been fairly treated by the insurance company, and, thinking it only fair that she should give the company a testimonial, she wrote them: "On February 15th my husband took out a policy with your company. Three weeks later he was killed suddenly. I think insurance is a fine investment."

But the reverse happened in Canton, Ohio.

The man's car had been destroyed in a fire. When he visited the insurance company's office to fill out the necessary forms, the manager told him he could have a new car.

"Not cash?"

"No, we'll buy you a new car. Where are you going?"

"Over to the Life Insurance Company, where I have a policy on my wife. This seems like a good system."

———•———

The agent for the casualty insurance company had certain questions to ask. "You travel in your car, I suppose?"

"I haven't a car," said the applicant.

"Ride a motorcycle or bike, perhaps?"

"No, I walk."

The agent shook his head. "Sorry, we don't insure pedestrians any more."

———•———

Another chap who is now a pedestrian told a friend, "Someone took my auto this morning."

"Call the sheriff."

"He's the one who took it."

———•———

On the dissenting side there is the man who didn't believe in insurance of any kind except fire insurance. He took out a $50,000 policy in the latter category.

"Why?" asked a company official.

"When I die, I know where I'm going."

———•———

The life insurance agent probed the customer's needs. "How about a straight life?"

The other looked sheepishly at the agent. "To tell the truth, I like to step out once in a while."

———•———

One person in every eight has an accident. The other seven have accident insurance.

———•———

It was a romantic moment for the doting husband. "Isn't this wonderful sitting here before the fireplace? Isn't that a swell fire?"

"Yes," said his wife, "but I'm sure going to miss the furniture."

————◆·◆————

The one form of insurance that reaches into all our lives is social security. But one alarmist feels such protection is menaced.

> Things have come to a pretty pass
> When war makes so many vital things scarce;
> Without giving men the ghost of a chance
> They'll take the zippers right off our pants,
> Thus heartlessly robbing men like me
> Of my hard won social security.

# CHAPTER 11

# Ambulance Chases Lawyer

THERE WAS a time in our legal history when the spoofers artfully insinuated that riding every ambulance was not an interne, but a lawyer. Today all that is changed. We have so many daily casualties that the ambulance now chases the lawyer. A man in Chicago was bitten by his own false teeth and consulted his attorney as to whether he could sue the dentist. Louis Durdy, of Pana, Illinois, dashed into a burning hotel and rescued a sleeping guest from a flaming mattress. Firemen walked in, seized the burning bedding, and tossed it out the window. It landed on the roof of an automobile parked outside. You guessed it. It was Mr. Durdy's car—and he was burned up, too!

Or take Bill Hilterbrand, of Springfield, Missouri. He was indulging in a bottle of soda pop at a filling station. Engrossed in conversation with a friend, Bill picked up the bottle and took a big swig. Only it wasn't soda pop. It was brake fluid. Naturally, that stopped Bill immediately.

Bob Forde, walking along the streets of Marysville, California, gave no particular thought to two men approaching him. Since they were walking so far apart, Bob decided to step between them. They were carrying a large sheet of window glass.

A spectator at a baseball game in Harrisburg, Pennsylvania, was using a wooden match to poke his ear when a foul fly ball struck him. The match was driven into his ear-drum. When he appeared in police court, the magistrate told him, "I can give you a hearing, except in the ear that was struck."

An army private, using an old style razor, was shaving in the barracks at an Arizona flying field. As it was a warm, humid day, the lad was devoid of clothing. When a fly punc-tured his rump, the soldier instinctively slashed at the fly and his razor made a sizable dent in his fundament.

At Bellevue Hospital in New York there is a special ap-paratus for removing billiard balls from the mouth. Each week someone is brought in who bet a friend he could hide one of the ivory balls in his mouth. And, while we frequently read about an automobile crashing into a train, in Hibbing, Montana, a train was struck on both sides by two different cars. All ten occupants of the two cars were injured.

George Lundgren, of Aurora, Illinois, was diapering his baby. Nothing unusual about that, but Mr. Lundgren liked to coo to the baby and there was an open safety pin in his mouth. He inhaled when he should have exhaled. The pin was removed from his throat at a nearby hospital.

Each year people design new and unusual ways of getting hurt. And as long as there are accidents, there will be casu-alty insurance companies. And where there are insurance companies . . . there are lawyers.

So many of these accidents today are attributable to the automobile that one poetic gentleman urges our return to the horse:

> Oh, horse, you are a wondrous thing,
> No horns to honk, no bells to ring.
> No license buying every year,
> No accidents that bring on fear.
> No sparks to miss, no gears to strip,
> No hitting people every trip;

No gas bills mounting up each day,
No mayhem, murder, on our way.
Your inner tubes are all okay—
We are relaxed and need not pray.

———•·•———

He walked on crutches. His wife couldn't understand it. "Four months ago, you were hit by the taxicab and last week the doctor said you're okay. So why are you still using the crutches?"

"My lawyer says I still need 'em."

———•·•———

In Morgantown, West Virginia, Mrs. Isabell Shaffer, suing the General Hospital, charged that, while she was being X-rayed there for a broken arm, she fell off the laboratory table and broke her leg.

———•·•———

When an elderly Polish-American workman, Stanley Kubierski, fell into a street excavation in Jersey City one night, he consulted lawyer Will Weiss.

"You have a good case," advised the lawyer. "There was no warning lamp. Your hip is injured. But before we could convince the judge and jury, you must obtain an X-ray picture. You understand?"

Kubierski said he did, so Weiss directed him to a radiologist. But Stanley never reached the radiologist's office. Instead, he hobbled along Newark Avenue until he found one of those photographic studios that specialize in Sunday afternoon Polish wedding portraits.

On Wednesday a picture of Stanley reached the lawyer. It was a studio pose. Stanley's long woolen underwear had dropped to his shoe tops. He was pointing his bare rump directly at the camera. A derby hat was atop his head and his handle-bar mustache drooped over the serious lines around his mouth. As he looked over his shoulder, the poignancy in his eyes seemed directed at tomorrow's courtroom with a wistful expression translatable only as "Please believe me, your honor."

The lawyer restrained his rising mirth. "This won't do, Stanley."

"But it is the picture, no?"

"It's not an X-ray picture, Stanley. I couldn't think of showing this picture to the judge."

"Why?"

"It would be disrespectful," said Will Weiss. "What would the judge think of us? Look, you have your hat on."

---

A careful driver will always give a woman half the road if he ever finds out which half she wants.

One male driver in Bridgeport insisted the lady in front of him signaled for a left-hand turn. "Your arm was well extended from the window," he insisted.

"What if it was?" she asked. "I had just come from the beauty parlor and I was waiting for the nail polish to dry."

---

When former Governor Harold G. Hoffman of New Jersey was the State Motor Vehicle Commissioner, he had to overrule a zealous assistant.

A pregnant woman had been denied an auto driver's license. The assistant had turned her down.

"Why?" asked Commissioner Hoffman.

"Because, Chief, the way I look at it, if a dame is careless one way, she'll be careless another."

---

George Burns, looking over his bank statement, spoke to his wife. "Gracie, what's this check stub, one pullover, $25? I don't want to sound like a cheapskate, but isn't that a lot of money for a pullover?"

"The man on the motorcycle said it was the regular price."

"You got it from a man on a motorcycle?"

"Yes, I went through a red light and he drove up and said, 'Pull over!'"

———•———

In Washington, D. C., police dropped charges against Stanley V. Baranauskas for driving through eight stop signs after he proved that he had been driving in the wrong direction in a one-way street and could not see the signs.

———•———

A farmer, who was a witness in a railroad case in Vermont, was asked to tell in his own way how the accident happened.

"Well, Jake and me was walkin' down the track and I heered a whistle and I got off the track; and the train went by, and I got back on the track and I didn't see Jake; but I walked along, and pretty soon I seen Jake's hat, and I walked on and seen one of Jake's laigs, and then I seen one of Jake's arms, and then another laig, and then over on one side was Jake's head, and I says, 'By cracky, something muster happened to Jake!'"

———•———

Two friends were discussing a reckless driver. "When the road turns the way he does, it's just a coincidence."

———•———

Some motorists think a locomotive only whistles at crossings to keep up its courage.

———•———

In a study of our life habits called "Queerespondence," Gurney Williams, alias the Professor, supplies the long-sought answer to a motorist's question.

Dear Prof: When the traffic light turns green, what length of time elapses before the driver in back of you blows his horn?— Norman H. Girk, Penn Yan.

Dear Norman: In File H-HW (Horns and Half-Wits) I find fairly complete data on this type of insanity. Reports show that the average driver leans on his horn approximately 1/1000 of a second after the light turns green, which is a shade longer than it takes the average woman driver to start a left turn after she has made what is laughingly called a hand signal.

———— • • ————

An Inquiring Reporter once stopped six chronic horn-blowers and asked them why they did it. The answers are significant.

1. "I dunno."
2. "Well, I thought the sap ahead must have run out of gas."
3. "The goon behind me started to blow his horn."
4. "Why, I always blow my horn at the jerk ahead. What's it for, anyway?"
5. "If I hadn't of, I might a been late at a party."
6. "Oh, did I blow the horn?"

———— • • ————

We can never forget a George Price cartoon showing three lawyers chasing an ambulance. Two of them are quite close to the vehicle as it speeds up the avenue. The third lawyer, an elderly chap, is puffing in the distance and being woefully left behind.

One of the lawyers closing in on the ambulance says to the other, "Murdoch has a fine legal mind but he fades in the stretch."

———— • • ————

"Pull over to the side," growled the big cop. As he approached the car now at the curb, he noticed the man at the wheel was a priest.

"There's no left turn permitted here, Father . . . so you can say for your penance five Our Fathers and ten Hail Marys."

A similar story comes out of Michigan. A young school-teacher was recently stopped in Detroit for driving through a red light and given a ticket to appear in traffic court the following Monday. She went at once to the judge, told him that she had to be at her classes then, and asked for the immediate disposal of her case.

"So," said the judge sternly, "you're a schoolteacher. That's fine, madam; your presence here fulfills a long-standing ambition for me. For years I have yearned to have a schoolteacher in this court. Now," he thundered, "you sit right down at that table over there and write 'I went through a Stop sign' five hundred times."

———— • ————

The lady driver had reached a rural road when she saw two telephone linemen climbing up separate poles.

"The fools," she said, "do they think I'm not used to driving?"

———— • ————

Pat O'Connor, one of the most astute insurance investigators in the east, has a little poem on his desk that serves as an object lesson in safety:

> My bonnie looked into the gas tank,
> The height of its contents to see.
> She lit a small match to assist her—
> Oh, bring back my bonnie to me.

———— • ————

A shrewd psychologist of Owensboro, Kentucky, was responsible for the placing of a box full of bright red flags on each corner of a busy intersection.

Above each box this sign warned daredevil citizens: "If you must cross against the red light, carry one of these flags and place it in the box on the opposite corner."

As predicted, fear of ridicule succeeded in putting a stop to those hair-raising dashes from curb to curb.

In short, pedestrians seem more concerned about "losing face" than losing a leg.

But if they would listen to some statistics of Leo Welch, Director of Safety Education, New Jersey Motor Vehicle Department, they might be less reckless. Says Leo:

"A live man pays twenty-five cents for a shave;
  It costs five dollars to shave a dead man in the morgue.
A woolen overcoat costs forty dollars,
  A wooden one costs four hundred.
A taxi to the theatre costs a dollar for the round trip,
  But one to the cemetery costs ten dollars for one way.
Stay alive and save your money.
  It's easy—drive carefully!"

During a casualty case, an overdressed gal was on the stand.

The insurance company lawyer lost patience over inconsistencies in her testimony. He turned on her, saying sarcastically, "And I suppose when the elevator started to fall, all your sins flashed before you?"

"Don't be silly," she said. "We only dropped eight stories."

Don MacGregor adds his contribution.

Two men finished their drinks at the tavern, said goodbye to their friends, and began the forty-mile drive to the city. After a while one of them observed, "We're gettin' closer to town."

"What makes you think so?" countered the other.

"Well," reasoned the first, "we're hittin' more people."

That the casualty insurance business is a source of steady legal profits can be proved by a cartoon in the *New Yorker,* drawn by R.J.D.

Outside the Bar Building two automobiles have collided with a resounding bang. There's a mad dash from the corridors as a bevy of lawyers rush forward to represent the drivers. Upstairs, in this lawyers' building, every office window is open and cards are being thrown down.

The lawyers would have had a field day if they had been in Cleveland when Mrs. Elmwood Mason drove her car straight through a red light, hitting eight other automobiles, a street car, and a truck on her way. Then she said, "I still think the light was green."

---

A candidate for the police force was being given a verbal examination.

"If you were by yourself in a police car and were pursued by a desperate gang of criminals in another car doing forty miles an hour along a lonely road, what would you do?"

The candidate looked puzzled for a moment. Then he replied: "Fifty."

---

The motion picture star, Pat O'Brien, asked his priest to bless his St. Christopher medal so that he'd be safe while driving.

The padre agreed but added, "Remember—the blessing is only good up to thirty-five miles per hour!"

---

Elsie M. Winchell of Media, Pennsylvania, knows that a definite casualty of every casualty case is the stenographer who has to prepare the case for court.

> On a dark, rainy night—there's no traffic light,
> Brakes screech with the blast of a horn;
> Two vehicles smash with a terrible crash,
> And, presto!—a lawsuit is born.
>
> The Statement of Claim says John Doe is to blame,
> The defendant with vigor denies it,
> The parties will bicker, the lawyers will dicker,
> —And the jury finally tries it.

I. D. Fendum, Esquire, says the plaintiff's a liar,
In suave, polite language, of course,
He files some New Matter, the record grows fatter,
And the battle is on, in full force.

The Statement is ended, then must be amended,
Or—"There's just a correction or two."
It is neatly redrawn, then as time marches on
'Tis rejected, or pencilled in blue.

With a weak, sickly grin, the poor steno digs in,
To grind out the umpteenth revision,
And, while typing furiously, conjectures curiously
What will be the final decision.

'Tis ever the same, be there trucks in the Claim,
Or merely two battered jalopies,
There's page after page—all learned and sage,
—And usually six carbon copies!

Nervous motorist Batista Linco, of Lambertville, New Jersey, explained he had been driving on 224 consecutive learner's permits over the past twenty-five years because he had flunked his first driver's test. He had been unsure of himself ever since, he said.

It was the busiest intersection of the city. Traffic, all that morning, had been excessively heavy. And there stood a sweet old lady holding everything up.

She beckoned to the traffic officer and he ambled over to unsnarl the traffic jam she was causing.

"Officer," she said, as he swooned, "I just want you to know that your badge number is the same as my favorite hymn."

A friend of ours caught in Manhattan traffic saw a little woman dash in front of a car. The driver stopped just in time. "Then," says our friend, "the traffic cop turned to the woman and said, 'Lady, that's *abusing* the privilege of being stupid!'"

But don't go away yet. Listen to this.

In Coeur d'Alene, Idaho, Deputy Sheriff Cliff Johnson, responding to an early morning call, went out to a narrow country road and broke it up between a couple of motorists who had been refusing for twelve hours to back up for each other.

A sign in Connecticut that has reduced the accident rate, reads:

> DRIVE LIKE HELL
> AND YOU'LL GET THERE.

———•—•———

The lawyer came over to the railroad station when his client sent a messenger and found a doctor setting the client's leg in splints. "How did you break your leg, Tom?" asked the lawyer.

"Do you see those six steps over there?"

"Yes."

"Well, I didn't."

Accidents can happen very easily. An elderly lady in Schenectady was electrocuted when she stepped on a bun.

The currant went up her leg.

Joe McGee in Newark was bitten by a dog and rushed to St. Michael's Hospital. The dog was taken to the Board of Health laboratories for examination.

Mrs. McGee came in a few days later with the news. "The dog is mad," she reported.

That riled Joe. "Why should the dog be mad? I didn't bite him. He bit me."

———•—•———

The lawyer was agreeable. "I'll defend you. Have you any money for trial expenses?"

The client answered, "Just a '49 Pontiac."

"O. K.," said the lawyer, as he jotted down some notes. "Now what are you charged with stealing?"

"A '49 Pontiac."

———•  •———

In Long Beach, California, two policemen checking a stolen car report, found the automobile parked in front of the owner's home. This was her bland explanation: "I guess the rain washed it clean—I didn't recognize it."

From Pittsburgh comes the report that Herbert Gibbs, a nightclub doorman, was given a jail sentence for taking a patron's car on his first day on the job. He didn't park the car until he reached Cleveland.

———•  •———

A railway supervisor received the following note from one of his foreman:

"I am sending in the accident report on Casey's foot when he struck it with the spike maul. Now, under *Remarks,* do you want mine—or Casey's?"

———•  •———

The very stout woman lost a thumb in a street railway accident. When the adjuster for the company called, she was emphatic in her demands. "I want $20,000 for that lost thumb."

"But, madam, that seems a lot of money for a thumb."

"Well, it isn't," she insisted. "It's the one I kept my husband under."

———•  •———

Judge Arthur C. Thomsen of Omaha, pondering a traffic damage suit, told the jury, "A careful driver ought reasonably to anticipate some vehicles making viatic use of the road." He then added with great satisfaction, "I have been waiting two years to get a case where I could use the word 'viatic.'"

"The Lord Chief Justice of England," declared Philip Guedalla, "recently said that the greater part of his judicial time was spent in investigation of collisions between pro pelled vehicles, each on its own side of the road, each sound ing its horn, and each stationary."

Authentic news misprint: "The motorist approached the coroner at 60 miles per hour."

In Troy, New York, Police Justice Thomas O'Connor complained that ten traffic violators had paid their fines with bad checks.

Just drivers whose cars and checks keep bouncing along.

The judge spoke sternly. "You're a menace to pedestrians. No more driving for two years."

The defendant whined, "But, your honor, my living depends on it."

"Quite true, but so does theirs," replied the judge.

The London *Daily Herald* once ran a descriptive headline:

CAR—CARESS—CARELESS—CARLESS.

Have you tried driving a car lately in Los Angeles? Then think of the plight of the pedestrians.

On the Eddie Cantor show, Parkyakarkus explained it accurately. "Los Angeles is so crowded that the only way to get on the other side of the street is to be born there."

The army doctor was examining a draftee. "Flat feet ever bother you?"

"Only once—in Brooklyn. One of them grabbed me for speeding."

A lawyer received the following letter from a client: "My husband got struck by an automobile, Number E-6843. If the owner is rich, sue him at once. John wasn't bruised any, but on your notifying me that you have brought suit, I will hit him in two or three places with a hammer."

———•———

The dealer met his bandaged customer.

"How could you have had an accident with that used car I sold you?"

The bandaged customer replied, "I couldn't put my hand out while I was pushing the car around the corner."

———•———

Famous last lines:

I had the right of way, but the other fellow had a truck.

None of us was driving when the accident happened. We were all in the back seat.

I admit, St. Peter, I was the nut that held the wheel.

The tires were loose but I was tight.

# CHAPTER 12

# Torts and Retorts

A TORT is a private or civil wrong or injury, arising independent of contract. The proper remedy is an action for damages.

The most famous tort of all occurs in the song, *Frankie and Johnny*, "He was her man, but he done her wrong."

There is a distinction between torts and crimes. If the wrongful act violates a private right, it is a tort. If it violates a public right, it is a crime. Frequently, the tort violates both private and public rights.

Ancient law invoked bodily punishment for many torts. The code of Hammurabi (2250 B.C.) stated, "If a man destroy the eye of another man, they shall destroy his eye." And in Cicero's day (*De Legibus*) the rule was *Noxiae poena par esto* (Let the punishment match the offense).

When the principal of a Topeka, Kansas, high school caught two students with ice cream cones in their pockets, he followed this principle. He didn't scold them. He simply made them leave the cones where they were.

A woman in Evansville was positive she had been wronged by a spiritualist and consulted a lawyer. "I was positively guaranteed," she said, "that at a seance they would bring back my husband to me. It was a fake. They said Egbert was in the room, but I didn't believe it."

"Why not?" asked the lawyer.

"Egbert never smelled of hot pastrami."

———— • ————

There's one woman in a rural area who is sure the local distributor of electrical ranges did her wrong. Her petition in law tells the story:

"Plaintiff alleges defendant represented this range would not become heated on the upper surface of the oven. That plaintiff, relying wholly upon defendant's representation, placed her bathtub in the kitchen near the range. That, upon emerging from the tub, plaintiff's foot accidentally came into contact with the soap upon the floor, and she was thus compelled to sit upon the range. That, although she arose therefrom in all diligence, she discovered she had been branded H-47 on her buttocks."

———— • ————

A woman in Rochester, New York, was sorely disappointed when the Appellate Division of the State Supreme Court upheld the judge's decision against her damage suit for injuries suffered in a fall, agreeing that "she might expect a barroom floor to be wet on Christmas Eve."

And in El Paso, Texas, the County Attorney considered a loaf of bread concocted by baker Dionicio Suarez, and ruled that it "did then and there contain added deleterious ingredient, to wit, a razor blade, which then and there rendered such article of food injurious to health."

———— • ————

A lawyer with a reputation as a Lothario was invited to dinner by a hostess who was slightly hard of hearing. He begged off. "I'm truly sorry," he said, "but I have to be in court early in the morning and tonight I'm going over the tort."

She beamed on him. "Why don't you bring the tart here with you?"

An aggrieved patron entered suit against a hotel owner, who called him on the 'phone and said indignantly: "There's some mistake. You were with us one night and allege that vermin kept you awake. Why, we haven't a single bug in our hostelry."

"Granted," said the other. "They're all married and have large families."

———•———

A complete textbook was written in a simple sentence by an elderly man in Birmingham, Alabama. His lawyer had just won a judgment in the old fellow's favor against the man who had defrauded him of $400. "You know, Mitchell," said the lawyer, "a judgment has teeth."

Mitchell pondered the complete poverty of his opponent. "What's it gonna bite on?"

———•———

Whether or not it had something to bite on did not deter the Franklin Credit School of Roanoke, Virginia, from suing Maurice J. Cleary in Albany, New York. Maurice was a student in its correspondence school, taking a course on how to operate a collection agency. Maurice overlooked an important part of the curriculum. He didn't pay his tuition bill. The school obtained a judgment against its alumnus.

———•———

After Frank Bacon's famous play *Lightnin'* became a solid hit on Broadway, a plagiarism suit was filed against him.

The plaintiff's lawyer bellowed, "We don't say that Bacon had actually stolen our entire play. But its vitals, its essence is ours." Here the lawyer placed his watch on the counsel table. "Like this watch. I might say, 'Has Bacon taken the outside?' Oh, no. He disguised the interior . . . but he has stolen the works."

Then Bacon drawled, as everyone in the courtroom laughed, "What has that got to do with the case?"

A law student described the whole subject of debt: A debtor is a man who owes money. A creditor is a man who *thinks* he is going to get it back.

Manny Kripelman, a cloak-and-suiter, was owed some money. But Manny did more than think he would be repaid. He decided a snappy collection letter was needed. After he had composed it meticulously, he still had doubts about the spelling and showed the letter to his wife.

"This is a fine letter, Manny. It is full of diplomacy and tact," she said. "There are only two infinitesimal corrections. Dirty is spelled with one *t* and there is no *c* in louse."

---

"Well, Uncle Joe," the real estate man said to an old man who had just paid the last instalment on a small farm, "I'll make you a deed to the farm now it's been paid for."

"If it's all the same to you, I wish you'd give me a mortgage on the place," said Joe.

The surprised real estate man protested that Uncle Joe didn't seem to know the difference between a deed and a mortgage.

"Well, mebbe not," said the other, "but I owned a farm once an' had a deed for it, an' the First National Bank had a mortgage, an' the bank got the farm!"

---

"Professor," asked the bright young law student, "could a blind man be made liable for his note payable at sight?"

"Son," retorted the professor, "that could only be brought out if the blind man was also given a hearing."

---

The landlord was showing the prospective tenant over the apartment. "The last people here damaged the rooms. Do you have any children?"

"No children."

"Any dogs or other pets?"

"No, sir. But I have an uncontrollable tendency to burp after a hearty meal."

———————

Another tenant, moving out, wanted to make sure there would be no subsequent legal action against him. As he handed the keys to the landlord, he said, "I had some boys collect a thousand cockroaches and a few mice."

"What?"

"It's in the lease. Says I must leave the premises the way I found them."

———————

Two lawyers fought over a question involving the limits of certain land and the riparian rights thereto.

"We lie on this side, your honor," one lawyer remarked with great emphasis.

"We lie on this side, your honor," interposed the other with equal vehemence.

At which his honor leaned back and observed, "If you lie on both sides, whom am I to believe?"

———————

In a tort action reported by Judge Leonard Hanower, the lawyer, on cross-examination, was attempting to find the hidden assets of the defendant, "Come, come, you must have other assets than your salary."

"None."

"You're a drinking man. Don't you have a case of liquor at home?"

"Yes."

"And what else do you have?"

"I have a case of rheumatism."

———————

A tort involving thousands of dollars came on appeal before Chief Justice Gummere of New Jersey's highest court.

After the plaintiff's lawyer had stated his case, Justice Gummere remarked, "I can't hear you."

The lawyer raised his voice, but again the justice said, "I told you I can't hear you."

Then the lawyer really let loose with his larynx. He could have drowned out a hundred cannon.

The justice called him to the bench. "You don't understand. I have no jurisdiction in this matter. In other words, I can't hear you."

———•—•———

He told the story to his lawyer. "Can I get back what I paid? I've been victimized." The lawyer said he would study the matter. And this was the client's story.

He had long desired to own a parrot and when he noticed on a pet shop . . . BANKRUPTCY SALE . . . he thought he might get one reasonably. Entering, he saw a gorgeous parrot in a cage. When the auctioneer put it up for sale he began bidding; higher and higher went the bids, but finally the parrot was his.

Bursting with pride of ownership, he walked out of the shop carrying the parrot in its shiny cage, when suddenly it occurred to him that perhaps the parrot couldn't talk. Back he ran and, holding the cage up to the auctioneer, demanded, "Say, does this bird talk?"

"Whothehell do you think was bidding against you all that time?" said the parrot.

———•—•———

Mefoosky tells about the time when he had an altercation on a golf course. He had taken Mrs. Mefoosky and the six little Mefooskys for a picnic in the country.

They had nestled in a quiet, green, shady spot when a special officer appeared. He looked at the fifth green, littered with paper cups and broken pieces of sandwiches, then exploded.

"This is no public park. You are on the fifth green of one of the most exclusive country clubs in America. The initiation fee alone is five thousand dollars, and the annual dues are twenty-five hundred. I have a good mind to arrest you for trespass."

Mefoosky looked up blandly. "With that kind of talk, how're you gonna get new members?"

———•—•———

Mefoosky knew he had been damaged when the golf ball hit him over the eye. He waited for the foursome to approach.

"I'll get a lawyer and sue you for five hundred dollars."

"Didn't you hear me yell 'Fore'?" asked one of the golfers.

"O. K.," said Mefoosky, "we'll settle for four hundred."

———•—•———

Here's how one potential action in tort was withheld. When a housewife sent her best colored luncheon cloth and two of the matching napkins to the laundry, they came back miserably faded. She stormed into the laundry and got into line at the complaint desk. When her turn arrived, the clerk informed her seriously, "If you'll bring in the remaining napkins, madam, we'll be glad to fade them to match the rest of your set."

———•—•———

Former Justice of the New York Supreme Court Arthur Eugene Sutherland told this story:

A wholesaler in Chicago sent a letter to a postmaster in a small town in southern Illinois, asking for the name of some honest local lawyer who would accept a collection case against a local debtor who had refused to pay his account. He got this reply.

Dear Sir:

I am the postmaster of this village and received your letter. I am also an honest lawyer and ordinarily would accept a case against a local debtor. But I also happen to be the person to whom you sold these unmerchantable goods. I received your demand to pay and refused to pay it. I am also the banker to whom you sent the draft drawn on the merchant, which I sent back with a notice that the merchant refused to pay. And if I was not, for the time being, substituting for the pastor of our Baptist Church, I would tell you just where to stick your claim.

———•———

A chap in England might have rushed into court to prove damages to his reputation. But he chose a more effective method.

An English lady, self-appointed supervisor of village morals, accused a workman of having reverted to drink because "with her own eyes" she had seen his wheelbarrow outside a public house.

The accused man made no verbal defense, but the same evening he placed his wheelbarrow outside her door and left it there all night.

———•———

"He persuaded me, Counsellor, to invest in a stud farm, never telling me that feeding apples to the nags was so expensive."

"Did they eat many apples?"

"Did they? The way he fed them apples you'd think they grew on trees."

———•———

A man walking along a city street fell through an open manhole and broke his leg. He engaged high-priced counsel who brought suit against the city for two thousand dollars and won the case. The city appealed to the Supreme Court, but again the lawyer won the decision.

By this time, the case had consumed two years. After the claim was settled the lawyer sent for his client and handed him a hundred dollar bill.

"What's this?" asked the man, looking at the hundred dollar bill.

"That's your damages after deducting my fee, the cost of appeal, and other expenses," replied the attorney.

The man looked at the hundred dollar bill again, turned it over and carefully scanned the other side. He then looked up at the lawyer and said, "What's the matter with *this* bill? Is it counterfeit?"

———◆ ◆———

"You should not have struck him," said the bystander to the taxi driver. The victim had picked himself up and had ducked into the courthouse.

"Oh, no?" said the cabby. "Imagine the noive of the guy. Says he's on his way to bankruptcy court and, instead of payin' me, invites me inside to be a creditor."

———◆ ◆———

Bankruptcy, as every lawyer knows, is where you put your money in your hip pocket and let your creditors take your coat.

———◆ ◆———

"No," said the cop to the drunk, "you can't sue the city. In fact, you're not crippled at all. You're walking home with one foot on the curb and one in the gutter."

———◆ ◆———

The judge was peeved. "I think a good many torts could be settled out of court."

The defendant spoke up. "That's what the plaintiff and I were trying to do when the cops butted in."

———◆ ◆———

"My lawyer thinks I can obtain redress," wrote the client to the automobile salesman. "But, personally, I'd be satisfied if you just repeated what you told me when you sold me this used car. I'm getting dreadfully despondent."

———◆ ◆———

After having a bowl of chowder and coffee at a restaurant of a well-known chain, a New York public relations man was charged ten cents for bread and butter, which he hadn't eaten. When he protested that he hadn't ordered the bread and butter, the waiter said he was sorry, it was orders from the chain officials. Our hero—and to us he is a hero—asked for the manager, who said the waiter was right. "Orders, sir, you know."

The man paid the dime, very ungraciously. Back at his office he wrote a letter in public relations patter to the chain owners, telling them they were losing good will by charging for bread and butter, willy-nilly. A few days later, he sent the company a bill for professional services—$5,000.

By return mail came a letter from the restaurant's Wall Street lawyers pointing out that the whole thing was absurd, since they hadn't ordered any public relations service.

Our hero shot off a one-sentence reply: "Well, I didn't order bread and butter."

P.S. At any of the chain's restaurants today, you get bread and butter, but—if you don't want it, you don't have to pay for it.

The Eastman Kodak Company of Rochester, New York, has an inflexible policy on pictures of nude subjects. If photographers enclose such pictures for finishing, the company refuses to return them lest they become subject to Federal Post Office censure. Transmitting indecent pictures is a crime.

A man in Bridgeport sent in some studies of nudity and, with them, a brace of carrier pigeons. "If you're the good sports I think you are, you'll develop my pictures." The pigeons came home two days later with the pictures.

Leaping from pigeons to pigs, the wife of Lord Chancellor Hardwick once asked his bailiff if he could procure for a state dinner a pig of such and such dimensions.

The bailiff burst into the drawing room where she was entertaining guests, announcing:

"I've been to the market, my lady, and I've bought a pig of exactly your size."

# CHAPTER 13

# *You Gotta Have Wile Power*

PSYCHOLOGY as an aid to legal adroitness was portrayed by Gene Fowler in his biography of William Fallon, *The Great Mouthpiece,* but the employment of courtroom psychology to win a law case is as old as the profession itself. Solomon's famous decision to divide a child in half takes high rank.

The Imam Abzenderoud wasn't popular in his native city with a certain Mr. Big, who framed the lad on a trumped-up charge. A lady of doubtful virtue asserted the Imam was the father of her unborn child. Abzend, claiming it wasn't so, hired a mouthpiece, too. In fact, he hired two of them—one for the courtroom and one outside the courtroom, the latter being a ventriloquist. When they put the pregnant lady on the stand, she was asked by Abzend's lawyer, "Who is the true father of the baby?"

Before the lady could "frame" an answer, there was a babyish squall emanating from her abdomen and a startled court heard the baby cry out another name than Abzenderoud's.

More than two thousand years later, the astute Alex Simpson was defending a client on a charge of rape. The scene was the Hudson County Court House in New Jersey. Rape has a non-legal definition, namely, "the wrong man." Its legal definition is serious and a lawyer is never too sure of his client's innocence. But this young lady on the stand did not appear to Alex Simpson to be a *virgo intacta*. There was something so wordly-wise about her that he reached his cross-examination in a climax both cynical and challenging. "You wouldn't leave his automobile and go behind the billboard. Oh, no, not you. You bit him, scratched him, defied him to carry you. And when you reached there, you doubled your body in a crouch and said, 'I prefer death to dishonor.'"

The witness reared up. "Did he tell you that? It's a damned lie. He didn't have to carry me at all."

Simpson was urbane and unctuous. "Thank you, my dear, that's what I wanted to hear you say." His client was acquitted.

In the days before fingerprints made it difficult for witnesses to lie about previous convictions for crime, I. Faerber Goldenhorn would invariably probe deep into the hidden life of a hostile witness. In the lawyer's hand would be cupped a piece of paper which he would covertly peek at. "Tell me, my good man, have you ever been in jail?"

The witness would squirm a while, then blurt out a record that was not known to Goldenhorn. And the paper in the lawyer's hand was usually a receipted household bill!

A lawyer, pleading the cause of a slightly injured four-year-old boy, took the child in his arms and held him up to the jury. The little fellow's tears cascaded down his cheek.

"Why are you crying, son?" asked the kindly judge.

"Because he pinched me," said the boy, pointing to his lawyer.

---

A man checked in at a prominent hotel in one of our large cities. At the desk, he said to the clerk, "Would you mind putting this hundred dollar bill in the safe? I'll pick it up in the morning. Hate to carry large bills around."

The clerk took the bill. Next morning when the guest asked for his hundred dollar bill, the clerk shrugged off the demand. "Hundred dollar bill? You never gave me a hundred dollar bill. Have you a receipt for it?"

"No," said the guest, "but I know I gave it to you."

"Sorry," said the clerk, "but your memory's at fault."

The guest walked down the street until he saw a lawyer's office. He went in and consulted the attorney, who said, "Tell you what, we'll use psychology. Pick up some friend who knows you; get another hundred dollar bill, and return to the same clerk. In the presence of your friend, ask the clerk if he'll put the hundred dollar bill away for you. Then you and your friend leave. You, alone, return in an hour. Say to the clerk, 'Let me have that hundred dollar bill now.' The clerk, knowing you have a witness, will hand over the money. Now find your friend, the witness, and go back to the hotel an hour later. Step up boldly and say, 'May I have the hundred dollars I gave you this morning while my friend was here with me?' You'll have the clerk trapped."

The psychology clicked. The guest got all his money back. He returned to the lawyer and told him how successful the advice was. "And now, what is your fee?"

"A hundred dollars," said the lawyer.

———•———

The famous artist consulted the lawyer. "What am I to do? The wealthy Mrs. Massacash commissioned me at five thousand dollars to paint her portrait. Now she refuses to accept it."

"Why?" asked the lawyer.

"A whimsical reason. Her precious Pomeranian doesn't recognize her. So she says it cannot be a good likeness."

The lawyer smiled. "Here's what you should do. Invite the lady to your studio on any pretext. Tell her you've made certain changes. Shortly before she arrives, rub a slice of bacon over her patrician face."

The artist followed instructions. The dog sniffed the bacon

and made desperate lunges to kiss the painted lips. "Now that," said the lady, "is more like me. See how Ting Ling adores me."

The artist came over to thank the lawyer. "It was indeed a bright idea."

"It was bright in Rabelais' time," said the lawyer. "Whenever Rabelais had an enemy, he used to rub a slab of liver against a female dog, then slyly deposit the liver in the coat pocket of his enemy. Within minutes every male dog in Paris would be jumping and snapping at Rabelais' enemy."

---

During Prohibition days a certain bootlegger was on trial. His face had all the features of the toper—the strawberry nose, the bloated jowls, and the complete attitude of W. C. Fields in one of his alcoholic routines.

His counsel resorted to an unusual defense—candor. Addressing the jury, he said, "Gentlemen, look at the defendant closely."

They all did so. "Do you really and truly think, gentlemen, that if the defendant had a bottle of whiskey in his possession, he would sell it?"

The jury didn't think so. The verdict? Not guilty.

---

Sometimes the client uses psychology in his own behalf. A fourteen-year-old boy was the defendant in a paternity suit.

His doting mother created a courtroom scene. She denounced the prosecutor. And with dramatic defiance she advanced on her son and shouted, "I'll show you how impossible and ridiculous this allegation is. I will ask the court to strip my boy and see that he is much too young for this sort of thing."

The son whispered in his mother's ear, "Don't do that, Ma. We'll surely lose the case."

After a young lawyer had talked nearly five hours to a thoroughly bored jury, his opponent in the case, a grizzled veteran of the legal cockpit, rose, smiled sweetly at the judge and jury and said, "Your honor, I will follow the example of my young friend who has just concluded, and submit the case without argument."

———

Abe Hummel was the slickest mouthpiece of an earlier New York era. He was once asked, "Isn't it the best policy for a man to do right and fear nobody?"

"No," said Abe. "Don't write and fear nobody."

———

A lawyer who is a trustee of a large endowment fund has the following story framed on his office wall where he can always see it.

For many years the keeping and administration of the funds of the old and famous Christ Church College of Oxford were entrusted to a banker in London.

One evening, as on many evenings during the school year, the banker was invited to dine with the treasurer of the college, Mr. J. Bull, the very popular canon at Oxford.

During the meal, the canon noticed that his guest, who usually was in the very best of humor and joking with the guests, was particularly preoccupied with religious ideas. He even asked about sins, their origin, their justification, absolution, etc.

Canon Bull, who had been thinking about his guest's peculiar behavior all evening, went down to the bank the very next morning to withdraw all the college's money, which was on deposit at the institution.

The following day the bank in question failed, but the college funds were saved, thanks to the treasurer, who was also a good psychologist.

———

Morris Fleishman recalls a case wherein an actress was testifying in New York in a suit for damages, and the cross-

examiner plotted to discredit all her testimony by proving
that she consistently lied about her age. She was fifty-two
but posed as being about forty. She didn't want to lie under
oath.

"How old are you?" the cross-examiner asked.

"I don't know," she said promptly.

"What! You don't know?"

"No. I have never had a birth certificate. I have never
looked up the record of my birth."

"But, Miss . . . ," the cross-examiner protested suavely,
"surely your parents told you how old you are. When did
they say you were born?"

"That," said the actress firmly, "is hearsay evidence and I
am sure you would not ask that it be admitted."

"But . . . but . . ." the cross-examiner sputtered.

The actress turned to the judge. "Am I right or wrong,
your honor?"

The judge grinned. "You are correct," he said.

———— • ————

A coroner testifying at a murder trial in Yakima, Washington, answered the attorney's question during cross-examination. "The thickness of human skulls, sir, varies with
individuals."

The lawyer forgot his manners. "How thick is your
skull?"

The coroner smiled. "Just a little thinner than yours."

———— • ————

Francis Rufus Bellamy recalls an amazing case of legerde-
main that happened some years ago in an Iowa courtroom,
where a railroad was being sued by a man who claimed that,
as a result of injury, he was a victim of nervous prostration
to such an extent that even a pin stuck in the top of his head
produced no pain—so paralyzed was his nervous system.

To the great surprise of the jury, the lawyer for the railway announced his own dismay at hearing that such a state was proof of neurasthenia, because he was in the same condition himself and evidently ought to be preparing to meet his Maker, not talking to a jury. Whereupon he took twelve needles from his coat lapel and stuck them in the top of his bald head. Thus bristling, he immediately conducted his case to a successful conclusion.

Not until some years later did he confess that he had almost been completely defeated, because he had stuck the last needle outside the area of the cocaine which had been injected in his scalp just before his appearance in court—and the pain had nearly unmasked him.

---

Mr. Bellamy also tells us that one of the most famous exposures of a manufactured story took place some years ago in a New York case, in which a little girl was allowed to tell her story in her own way—a very damaging story to the opposing side. She was a prepossessing little girl and made a great impression on the jury. The opposing lawyer did not even cross-examine her. "Jane," he said pleasantly, "tell it to us all over again, that's a good child." And she repeated it word for word from the beginning. She was letter perfect—and obviously so.

---

Jim Watson, one time U. S. Senator from Indiana, encountered a flair for courtroom "psychology" in an explosive lady client he represented. She was extremely difficult to control all during the trial.

The opposing side had two lawyers while Senator Watson stood alone for his client.

He felt a tugging at his sleeve in the midst of his direct examination of a witness. It was his client, who whispered, "We should get another lawyer for our side."

"Why?"

"On their side," exclaimed the lady, "when one is doing the talking, the other is doing the thinking. While on our side, when you're talking, there's no one thinking."

---

Six young housewives living in the same apartment building fell into a dispute of such magnitude that it resulted in their being haled into court. When the case was called they all made a concerted rush for the bench and, reaching it, broke into bitter complaints at the same moment.

The judge sat momentarily stunned, as charges and countercharges filled the air. Suddenly he rapped for order.

When quiet had been restored, the patient magistrate said quietly, "Now, I'll hear the oldest first."

That closed the case.

---

The primary purpose of cross-examination is to bring out the truth. But danger always lurks in the witness. Sydney Smith once said, "The best way of answering a bad argument is to let it go on." But when should the tap be closed against the "drip?"

Some years back Eddie Smith, a great trial lawyer, represented the Public Service Corporation in an action that resulted when a company vehicle backed into a horse-drawn junk wagon. Frank J. V. Gimino, a worthy legal opponent, represented the junk man.

Smith had a technique of bullying and smearing hostile witnesses. He employed all his savagery on a surprise witness produced by Gimino. This witness told a straight, eyewitness story. He had been at the scene, described the accident, and gave his opinion on how badly the horse had been injured.

On cross-examination, Smith snarled, "What do you know about horse injuries? You're not a veterinarian, are you?"

"No."

Again Smith sneered. "That means that you only know a

horse from a jackass when you see one. Is that it?"

The witness was polite, but his answer threw the courtroom into such laughter that Smith and his case had to run for cover. "Yes, sir, I think so," he said. "For instance, I'd never take you for a horse."

––– • • –––

Another example that proves the danger of the overbearing or smart-aleck approach in cross-examining a respected witness occurred in a case in Chicago.

In a suit for damages on account of personal injuries sustained in an automobile accident, counsel for the plaintiff had tried unsuccessfully to cast doubt on the expert testimony offered by a physician retained by the defendant. Toward the end of the cross-examination the attorney became rather sarcastic.

"You say you are familiar, Doctor, with the symptoms of concussion of the brain?"

"I am," replied the physician grimly.

"Well, if you and I were riding in an automobile which ran into another automobile and our heads were violently bumped together, isn't it your opinion that we would suffer concussion of the brain?"

"My opinion is," replied the doctor, deliberately, "that I would, but you couldn't."

––– • • –––

In his *Thesaurus of Anecdotes* (Crown Publishing Company, New York), Edmund Fuller gives us another insight into client's psychology.

One of the first clients of a criminal lawyer handed him a large bill as a retainer. The client insisted that he had been framed: "This guy says he felt my hand in his pocket. He's a liar. I've been a pickpocket for twenty-four years and no man ever felt my mitt in his kick."

When the man departed the lawyer felt for the precious

bill. No bill. He hunted through all his pockets and was crawling under the desk when his client returned. Handing the lawyer the bill, he said, "I wanted you to have your heart in this case. You can see for yourself the guy's a liar."

———•—•———

A young lawyer who should go far in the profession was asked during his bar examinations:

"Mrs. Smith, who has a letter of introduction from a very good friend of yours, gives your firm a check for $100,000 and asks you to advise her as to how she should invest her money. The letter of introduction states that Mrs. Smith is a widow, but gives no other information. What do you consider the ten most important questions you should ask her in order to obtain sufficient background to advise her?"

The young lawyer answered, "Why ask ten questions when one will do? 'What are you doing about dinner tonight?' "

———•—•———

A wise old Scot, who was a judge, was once asked to settle a dispute between two brothers over inheritance of a large estate. The judge's decision is historic: "Let one brother divide the estate, and let the other brother have first choice."

———•—•———

The owner of the factory called his attorney. "It's important. Rush over," he said.

When the lawyer got there he found that a sit-down strike was in progress. "How am I going to get them out of the plant without trouble?" the owner asked.

The attorney knew how to cope with the situation. Within an hour the factory owner came out to greet the strikers. "Boys, my lawyer says you can sit down as long as you want. But why not feel at home? I've got cots here. Plenty of liquor. And we've got some cuties coming over from Danceland in a few minutes."

The joint was jumping two hours later, when the strikers' wives arrived, tipped off by anonymous 'phone calls from the lawyer's office.

It required only ten minutes to clear the factory.

---

William Jennings Bryan's dad was Judge Silas Bryan. One night several hams were purloined from the Bryan smokehouse.

Next day a neighbor came over to sympathize. "I hear, Jedge, someone stole some hams from you."

"Keep quiet about it," pleaded Judge Bryan. "You and I are the only ones who know about it."

---

A man in Somerville, New Jersey, when he received an eviction notice from his landlord, rushed to his lawyer's office.

"Under the rules of the Federal Rent Control Act, you have certain rights," said the lawyer. This is the note his client was advised to write to his landlord:

"Dear Sir:
  I remain.
   Yours truly,
    John Deranden."

# CHAPTER 14

# *Jestice of the Peace*

HIS COURTROOM is often a homespun country parlor or a tiny office off Main Street where the furnishings are as sparse as the amount of law he knows. But he sits there, does the justice of the peace, a true protrait of a vanishing day in America when equity was a matter of whim and caprice. The creaking chairs, the battered desk, the ancient law book that must find citations for nonexistent causes—all these are unforgettable parts of our Humor Americana. In Indiana, he said to the witness, "If ye're not keerful, yer'll be committed for perjury. Yer just told the Court yer had only one brother, but yer sister has just sworn that she has two." In Idaho, he told the defendant's lawyer he didn't want to hear his side of the case. "Every time I hear both sides it gets dam' confusin.' "

Yes, the old justice of the peace is on his way out. New restrictions are gradually closing in on him that the law may be unfolded in more formal and dignified setting. But the old justice will live in our memory.

"The justice of the peace," wrote Albert E. Sherlock, of the Denver bar, "arrived in this country with the Mayflower. He had been created in the year 1360 when statute 34 (Edward III) appointed one lord and with him three or four of the most worthy in the county, with some learned in the law . . . to keep the peace and try felonies and trespasses at the king's suit."

As the years passed and the authority of the justices widened, usually without legislative sanction, their system of fee collections and their unholy alliances with collection agencies and instalment houses brought on constant criticism. Instead of being the local Solomon, our justice of the peace was usually Dogberry.

But he had a flair for the unusual verdict; the decision that seemed to float before him until bang went the gavel and impulse became a substitute for justice.

"Perfesser," whined the old justice of the peace in upper New York State, "I sure hate to see you here in my courtroom. But you're charged with being drunk and disorderly. How do you plead?"

The professor rose to dignified heights. "I am not narcotized as DeQuincey was; I am not so profligate as Byron was, nor intemperate as was Robert Burns—"

"Hold it, Perfesser," cried out the justice, "they'll have their own hearing when we pick 'em up."

———•———

It might have been proper for Shakespeare in *King Lear* to cast certain legal doubts in the words: "A man may see how this world goes with no eyes. Look with thine ears: see how yond justice rails upon yond simple thief. Hark, in thine ear; change places; and, handy-dandy, *which is the justice? Which is the thief?*"

But, when the law enforcement officers in Connecticut dragged in a widely-sought criminal, they hustled him into a rural courtroom while awaiting the arrival of an important official from the federal attorney's office. The justice of the peace moved around his courtroom making everyone feel sociable.

Then the federal attorney dashed in and greeted the officers. It was a long-awaited chance to berate the criminal for his many lawless deeds. The only interruption to the tirade came from the arresting officer. "Counsellor," he said, "all your words are true. But you're not addressing them to the culprit. This little fellow you're bawling out is the justice of the peace."

———•———

A justice of the peace in a small New England town was called upon to perform his first marriage ceremony. After he had struggled through the ordeal, the young couple continued to stand before him as if expecting some further rite.

Whereupon the justice rounded off the ceremony with a religious turn, "There, there, it's all over! Go and sin no more!"

———•———

Another old justice was rushed to a coroner's inquest at the county seat. The victim's body had been fished out of the river.

In his pockets had been found a fully loaded gun and a ten dollar bill. The justice was now ready for his decision.

"The court says this man came to his death by accidental drowning. I also find him guilty of carrying concealed weapons. The fine will be ten dollars."

———•———

When Lloyd Fisher was Prosecutor of Hunterdon County, New Jersey, he was called to a justice's home where a young farmhand was being booked, charged with committing arson.

It was to be a preliminary hearing, but the old justice showed signs of holding the trial right there and then.

"But your court is one of limited jurisprudence," Fisher protested. "All you can do is remand this young fellow for grand jury action." The boy's lawyer agreed with the prosecutor.

*"There, there, it's all over! Go and sin no more!"*

"Don't tell me what I can try and what I can't try," said the justice. "I know what arson is. We can try it in this court, and let's start now because Linda'll be likely callin' me to supper in an hour."

Reluctantly, Fisher presented the evidence. The young man's attorney entered rebuttal. A half hour later the old justice banged his gavel.

"The court's ready to announce the verdict. I find the

*"Thirty days, and fifty dollars, and* the defendant must post a bond to support the baby until it is eighteen. *It's high time we stamped out arson in this county!"*

defendant guilty of arson. I sentence him to serve thirty days in the county jail; pay a fine of fifty dollars, *and he must post a bond to support the baby until it is eighteen.* It's high time we stamped out arson in this county."

———•—•———

A justice of the peace in Oregon proved he could echo the dog in Lewis Carroll's *The Mouse's Tail.* (" 'I'll be judge, I'll be jury,' said cunning old Fury.")

According to C. R. Wade of Bandon, Oregon, this justice presided in a frontier district. He always wore his hat in the courtroom, a pipe jutted out from his jaw, and he kept his feet propped up on his desk.

The defendant stood before him in a preliminary hearing. The 'phone rang. It was the district attorney. He was delayed at the county seat and would the justice represent the State of Oregon at the hearing?

When the hearing got under way a question from defense counsel bolted the justice of the peace upward. Waving his hat and his pipe high over his head, he bellowed, "I object. On behalf of the State of Oregon, I object to the question."

Then resuming his seat, he slapped his hat back on his head and thrust his pipe in his mouth at a belligerent angle. He raised his feet on the desk and now his features softened. He was in deep meditation for a moment more before he spoke. "Objection sustained."

———•—•———

Another justice impaneled a constable's jury to hear a case involving personal property. After all the evidence was in and both sides had been heard, he addressed the jury. "The time has now arrived when the court must instruct you. If you think the plaintiff has told the truth, you must find for him. On the other hand, if you believe the defendant, you must render him the verdict."

The old chap cleared his throat and looked pompously at

them. "But . . . if you agree with me that they're both damned liars, well, frankly, I don't know what in hell you can do about it."

———•·•———

At another preliminary hearing, the justice of the peace glared at the defendant. "You're charged with forgery, Horace? How do you plead?"

"Not guilty. You know, Judge, I can't even write my own name."

"That doesn't enter into it, Horace. You're held for the grand jury. You're not charged with writing your own name."

———•·•———

"How can I marry you?" asked the vinegary justice in his ancient sitting room, which also served as courtroom. "This license doesn't have the date on it."

The young couple showed their disappointment. "Can't you write the date in?" asked the man.

"Not me," said the old fellow. "You go back to the Town Hall and get it straightened out."

"But it's nearly five o'clock," protested the man.

"You'll still have time."

The man raced back to the Town Hall. The clerk was preparing to leave, but he wrote the date in.

The old justice looked it over. "H'm," he said, "the clerk plumb forgot to put in the girl's name."

"But I can tell you her name. Or she can tell her name and you can write it in."

"Who, me?" The old fellow shook his head. "I don't tamper with official papers."

"But we've got to be married today. And the clerk will have gone."

"Not if you hurry," admonished the J. P.

Again the man scurried over to the Town Hall. The clerk

was halfway down the road when the bridegroom pleaded with him to return and fill out the license properly.

But again there was a hitch. "The license doesn't have the Town seal. No good without it, son."

"Please, Judge, I'll have it put on later."

"Oh, no; wouldn't be legal."

"Look, Judge, we have to be married. The clerk has gone home. The office is locked up. Don't you understand?"

"Here's his address, son. Might prevail on him to open up the office."

The prospective bridegroom found the clerk at home. "Please come back and put the seal on. I'll pay for your extra trouble."

The Town Clerk returned to the office and slapped the seal on.

"Wa'al, now, everythin' looks jake," said the old fellow. He proceeded with the ceremony. "I now pronounce you man and wife."

Then for the first time he noticed the four-year-old boy in the room. "Whose child is that?"

"Ours, Judge," said the bridegroom.

"You mean . . . you had the child before . . ."

"Yes, before we were married."

The old fellow puckered his face. "Wa'al, of course, you're married now. But, you realize, this child is a technical bas-tard."

"That's odd," spoke up the bridegroom, "that's just what the Town Clerk said you were."

———— • • ————

The lawyer for the plaintiff had finished his argument, and counsel for the defense stepped forward to speak, when the justice of the peace interrupted. His eyes were wide open, and filled with wonder and admiration at the skill of the plaintiff's lawyer.

"Defendant need not speak," he said. "Plaintiff wins."

"But your honor," said the attorney for the defendant, "at least let me present my case!"

"Well, go ahead, then," said the justice wearily.

The lawyer went ahead. When he had finished, the justice gaped in even greater astonishment.

"Don't that beat all!" he exclaimed. "Now defendant wins!"

———•·•———

Harry Uhlfelder of Long Beach, New York, gives us this: It was the justice's first day in office. The two lawyers, representing each side, stood before him.

"Judge," said one of the attorneys, "I move that this petition be dismissed."

The old man looked around the courtroom. "Anybody second the motion?"

———•·•———

Another startling pronouncement issued from the lips of a J. P. in eastern Tennessee.

"I will hold the case under advisement until Monday, when I will render a judgment for the plaintiff."

———•·•———

Out in Nevada a mining claim case was pending before a certain old-time western judge with a reputation for a rather rough and ready brand of justice. One morning his honor made the following remarkable statement.

"Gentlemen, this court has in hand a check from the plaintiff in this case for $10,000 and a check from the defendant for $15,000. The court will return $5,000 to the defendant, and then we will try this case strictly on its merits."

———•·•———

In rural Iowa, three witnesses testified before a justice of the peace that they saw the defendant walking down the road with the stolen hog.

The defendant produced ten witnesses who testified they

had not seen the defendant walking with any hogs that day.

"The defendant wins," announced the justice, "by the greater weight of evidence. Three saw him with the stolen hog, and ten didn't see him."

———•–•———

Ralph E. Shannon relates an epic of taciturnity.

Sam Russell, justice of the peace in Crawfordsville, Iowa, was a reticent man. One day a saleslady breezed into his residence and inquired if his wife was at home.

"No, she ain't home," the justice said.

"Do you mind if I wait?" the visitor asked.

"Nope, have a chair."

After a full hour of waiting, the woman asked, "Where is your wife?"

"She went out to the cemetery."

"How long do you think she'll be gone?"

"Well, I don't know," said the justice deliberately, "but she's been out there eleven years now."

———•–•———

Some justices are great sticklers for legal formalities. Judge Walker was particularly so. One day a veteran of World War II was brought in as a witness. The judge told him to hold up his right hand.

"Can't do it, your honor."

"Why not?"

"Got shot in that arm, sir."

"Well, then, hold up your left."

"Got shot in that arm, too, sir."

"Then," said Judge Walker, "hold up your leg. No man can be sworn in this court, unless he holds up something."

———•–•———

A justice of the peace had ruled against O'Brien. He paid the judgment but demanded a receipt.

"Why? We've entered it in the court record."

O'Brien insisted. "I want a receipt."

"Why so persistent?"

"Because when I get to heaven and St. Peter asks me if this judgment has been paid and I say, 'Yes,' he'll ask me for the receipt and I'll be damned if I'll tramp all over hell looking for you."

———•—•———

Under our system of jurisprudence anyone having knowledge of the facts in a court case may step before the judge and offer his testimony, as *amicus curiae,* friend of the court.

A federal attorney one night walked into the courtroom of a justice of the peace where two felons were being given a preliminary hearing. He spoke to the justice. "I have some facts on these two men. So, really, I'm here as *amicus curiae,* if you wish to hear me later."

As the hearing developed, the old justice seemed perplexed. His curiosity finally overpowered him. He motioned to the attorney to come forward. "Who's that fellow you say you represent?"

———•—•———

Down near the Arkansas-Texas boundary line, a man charged with stealing an automobile and killing a man during a holdup, was captured and brought before the justice of the peace.

"We got two kinds of law in this court, mister—Texas law and Arkansas law. Which'll you have?"

The prisoner took counsel with himself. "I'll take Arkansas law."

"Then," said the justice, "I discharge you for stealing the auto and order you put to death for killing the man."

"Just a minute, Judge," protested the prisoner. "A while ago, I was too hasty. If you don't mind, I'd like to switch to Texas law."

"It's your constitutional right," said the justice. "So under the Texas law I discharge you for killing the man, but order you put to death for stealing the auto."

———•—•———

"I can't convict you on the evidence," said another rural justice, "but I'm gonna fine you five dollars, anyway."

"What for?"

"Contempt."

"Contempt of court? I haven't done or said anything that could be construed as contempt for this court." The defendant spoke calmly.

"You don't understand," said the justice. "It isn't your contempt of the court; it's the general contempt I have for you."

———•—•———

Up in the mountain country of eastern Kentucky, they asked the old justice of the peace to say a few kind words over the body of a character known locally as a gambler, two-fisted drinker, and promoter of cock-fights.

The old "jedge" got up with great dignity and, without wasting time or words, said: "We come to bury Uncle Jed. He growed good tobaccer and he chawed it. He raised good chickens and he fit 'em. He held good cuyards and he played 'em. He made good likker and he drunk it."

Then he paused impressively, and concluded: "Of sich is the kingdom of heaven."

CHAPTER 15

# Don't Make a Will
# —It's a Dead Give-Away

BECAUSE you can't take it with you, millions of people yearly write out a last will and testament. Not the late Percy Hurst, of London. He spent a great part of his time and money conducting a one-man crusade against lawyers, telling the people in pamphlets and philippics that the legal profession was a bunch of old so-and-so's. When he died the heirs to his $200,000 estate got into a series of wrangles. Lawyers had to apportion the estate.

Maybe that's why at Gray's Inn, London, the barristers used to warble:

> Now this festive occasion our spirit unbends,
> Let us never forget the profession's best friends.
> So we'll send the wine around and a nice bumper fill
> To the jolly testator who makes his own will.

———•·•———

As Jerome Beatty pointed out in an excellent article ("A Will of Your Own"), "Most husbands, no matter how kind and considerate, punish their widows cruelly when they die. Fewer than four out of ten persons who own property have wills, and when men and women die without a will they usually leave a perfect hell to remember them by." The answer, of course, is to make your will today in the presence of a competent attorney. For where there's a will, there's a caveat, the legal restrainer imposed by the court until your last testament is probated.

The hell that Jerome Beatty indicates cropped up in a will case in Tallahassee. Relatives filed a caveat hoping to break the will. The witnesses said, "When Martin died, his wife had him laid out in light socks, rubber-soled shoes, and a suit of thin, flimsy material."

"Why did you do this, ma'am?" asked the considerate probate judge.

"If you knew Martin as I did, Judge, you'd know where he was goin' when he died. And I loved him enough to make him comfortable."

The judge sustained the will.

———•———

A man with an $8,000 estate, planning to leave all to a devoted wife, forgets to make a will. The widow receives about $1,866 instead of $5,600. Why? Our laws take it for granted when there is no will that the children must be provided for. So, in most states, two-thirds of the estate goes to the children to be held in trust until they come of age. They can't give any of this money to their mother.

Mother's only solution might be seeking a new mate who has a few odd dollars. In Montgomery, Alabama, a local marble works had been commissioned by a widow to carve on her late husband's monument, MY SORROW IS MORE THAN I CAN BEAR.

When the widow discovered how little was the gravy left in the pot, she quickly acquired another mate. Returning to the monument works, she asked the manager to add one more word to the epitaph—ALONE.

———•———

A man of considerable means had no relatives. But when he made out his will he also left special instructions for the undertaker in the event of his death.

In due time, the funeral took place—at four o'clock in the morning, in accordance with the undertaker's instructions!

Just four friends managed to drag themselves out of bed to attend the funeral at that unearthly hour. But they were well repaid for their trouble, for, when the lawyer's letter was opened, it was found to provide for an equal division of the estate of the deceased among those who attended his funeral.

The value of the estate was $400,000.

———•—•———

William F. McDermott has assembled some oddities in last wills and testaments.

A young lady in Kentucky showed rare sentiment by directing that tobacco be planted over her grave and that the weed, nourished by her dust, be smoked by her bereaved lovers.

Five hundred dollars was willed to the widow of an old farmer, who facetiously provided that double that amount be paid to her second husband, adding, "Him that gets her will deserve it."

As a boy, young Valentine Tapley swore that if Lincoln were elected he would never shave, with the result that he grew the longest beard in the world, some twelve and a half feet long by the time he died at the age of eighty. Then, fearful that his grave might be robbed for his whiskers, he provided that his body be sealed in an unbreakable tomb.

"Roll out the barrel" was the theme of a bibulous individual's will which provided that his friends should, at his expense, roll a barrel of beer to the cemetery and consume it on his grave.

———•—•———

There was a little lawyer man,
Who gently smiled as he began
Her dear husband's will to scan;

And thinking of his coming fee,
He said to her quite tenderly,
"You have a nice fat legacy."
Next morning, as he lay in bed
With bandages on his smashed-in head,
He wondered what-in-'ell he said.

---

A resident of Los Angeles received one dollar from the estate of his wife, "for the purpose of buying bullets for his gun, and with the suggestion that he shoot himself."

---

Abe Abramowitz was dying. His wife stood at the bedside, jotting down Abe's last wishes.

"The Oldsmobile I give to my oldest son, Dave."

"Why not to Solly? He could use it in his business."

"All right, give it to Solly. One-third of my A.T.&T. stock to Morris."

"Why not to Sammie? Morris would squander everything in a month."

"All right, give it to Sammie. My jewels, except for what you want, should go to Miriam."

"Miriam hates jewelry. Give it to Sylvia."

Abe was now peeved. Propping himself up, he rasped at his wife, "Hannah, who is dying? You or I?"

---

The aged wine dealer of Damascus knew the end was approaching. He had made out his will, but he thought additional advice should be imparted to his four sons gathered at the bedside.

"This is farewell. My will takes care of you all equally. Just remember this about the wine business. You've seen me pour water into wine and you might have the wrong impression that it is made of water only. Let me assure you with my last breath that you also need grapes."

A cartoon by Vanselew shows the lawyer in his office reading the will to a bevy of grasping, hungry relatives.

The lawyer has given each of them a shovel, as he chortles, "What a sense of humor! He buried it all somewhere in Texas and left each of you a shovel."

———•——•———

In nineteen states and Alaska, a will written in your own handwriting, signed and dated, but not witnessed, is legal if the court thinks you have been coherent in expressing your last wishes.

But wills have been broken on trivial technicalities. In Georgia a man lay dying on a hospital bed in the middle of a room. He prepared his will. Witnesses were at hand, but the only convenient writing space for them to sign their names was on a chest of drawers against the wall, six feet behind the bed.

The court ruled that the witnesses were concealed from the dying man and therefore were actually not in his presence as the law required. The will was not upheld.

In Sydney, Australia, there's a perplexed man today. He is tattoo artist Alex Chater.

He has had his will tattooed on his back. It's a simple statement . . . "I leave everything to my wife . . ." but he forgot one elemental fact. He is not a contortionist. He has his will on his back, but he can't sign it.

———•——•———

There are three tombstones in a family plot near Niagara Falls, Ontario. Here is the inscription on the center one:

"Here I lie between two of the best women in the world, my wives. But I have requested my relatives to tip me a little toward Tillie."

———•——•———

At an examination for admission to the bar of Ohio, the examiner propounded this question, "A great many years ago there lived a gentleman named Lazarus who died possessed of chattels, real and personal. After this event, to whom would they go?" The student replied, "To his administrators and heirs." "Well, then," continued the examiner, "in four days he came to life again; inform us, sir, whose were they then?"

A lawyer, hearing about the question, offered his "off-the-cuff" opinion.

"Since Lazarus died without a will, his property would revert to his heirs. The law gives no man the right to die for four days and then come to life again. Legally, Lazarus could not rise. I have no doubt the Supreme Court would decide that Lazarus who rose was not the Lazarus who died; he was a new Lazarus. The new Lazarus would, of course, feel within himself that he was the old Lazarus and go around bothering his legal friends talking about his legal wrongs; but every lawyer would leave him as quickly as possible, saying in parting, 'It's a hard case; but if your heirs can prove your death and they came in legally under the statute, there is no way to make them disgorge. All you can do is this—you're a young fellow, about sixty, hire out as a clerk, try to save something from your salary so as to go into business again. Build up a great estate and perhaps your heirs will recognize your identity.' "

———◆———

Proof of death is legally of great importance. G. W. Barham, of Blytheville, Arkansas, recalls a case where an administratrix died before she was able to sue a railroad for the death of her husband.

A substitution of administrator was sought from the court. Defense counsel said there was no proof before the court that the administratrix was dead.

The judge turned to plaintiff's counsel and asked, "What proof have you she is dead?"

The attorney's answer was strictly and legally cautious. "I don't know that she is dead. I only know she was buried."

———•———

Lawyer, reading client's last will and testament to circle of expectant relatives: "And so, being of sound mind and understanding, I spent every damn penny I had before I died."

———•———

Simple language quite often speaks the greatest prayer.

In Floyd, Virginia, a woman was making a deathbed request: "I don't want one of them little shirt tail shrouds and have to be always backing out of the presence of my Lawd!"

———•———

The sweet and amiable old lady accosted the deputy surrogate in the courthouse. "Where is the court of reprobates?"

"You mean the probate court. It's right through that door."

She smiled. "My husband died detested and left an infidel to the will."

The deputy pondered the translation. "Do you mean intestate? That he didn't have a will? An addition to a will, lady, is a codicil. I'm afraid your bereavement has you puzzled."

"Maybe it has. But this is the place, isn't it, where you apply to be the executioner?"

———•———

The case concerned a will, and an Irishman was a witness. "Was the deceased," asked the lawyer, "in the habit of talking to himself when alone?"

"I don't know," was the reply.

"Come, come, you don't know, and yet you pretend that you were intimately acquainted with him?"

"The fact is," said Pat angrily, "I never happened to be with him when he was alone."

*"And so, being of sound mind and understanding, I spent **every** damn penny I had before I died."*

For the greater part of an hour both sides argued with the court over the admissibility of a question to the witness.

The court called a short recess during which counsel dug into the citations in a hundred books.

It was a will case and the estate was considerable. Finally the court overruled the objection. "The question may be asked the witness."

The witness was now in a quandary. "What was the question again?"

The court stenographer read the question once more. "What did the testator say just before he signed the will?"

And the witness answered, "Nuttin'."

---

"Make out my will?" said the gay old rounder. "I've spent every dollar I've ever had. All I can leave is the earth."

---

"Did your father-in-law remember you when he made out his will?"

"He sure did," answered the other old rounder. "He didn't leave me a cent."

---

It was his dying wish and his wife leaned closer to catch the last words. "If you have a desire to remarry, pick John Ferndotan."

"Why?" she asked.

He gasped it out. "I've never forgiven him for trading me that broken-down Chevrolet twelve years ago."

---

The annals of crime have many a case of a wealthy man, dying intestate, whose widow, to insure all the estate for herself, created a forged will.

Such a woman persuaded her gardener to impersonate her dying husband. She promised him an ample fee, gave him all the instructions, and then covered him up to his ears in blankets when the lawyer arrived to draw up the will.

The gardener began the bequests. "To my dear wife one half of all I die possessed of."

"And the residue?" asked the lawyer.

"To my faithful gardener of many years' service, Lewis Arburton, I bequeath the remaining half."

———•—•———

She was indignant when she found her husband burning the love letters he wrote her years ago. "Oh, Harry, how could you? Have you lost all sentiment?"

"No, darling. Hold everything. I'm doing this for your own protection. When I die I don't want anyone attacking my will on the ground that I was always nuts."

———•—•———

There have been some satiric observations on our last days in this world. Dr. Robert T. Norris said, "I hate funerals and would not attend my own if it could be avoided, but it is well for every man to think what sort of collection of mourners he is training for his final event."

The son of Lady Montagu (you'll remember her as saying, "I am reconciled to being a woman in the knowledge that I'll never be married to one") when he made out his will, wrote:

"To Lord A——, I give nothing, because I know he'll bestow it on the poor."

———•—•———

Mr. Sanborn of Medford, Massachusetts, willed that his skin be made into drumheads and that on June 15th each year on Bunker Hill at sunrise, the drum should be beaten to the tune of "Yankee Doodle."

———•—•———

Those who like the salty flavor of Irish stories should read the collection of Kerry tales by Bryan MacMahon (*The Lion Tamer*, E. P. Dutton & Co., Inc., New York).

In one yarn called "The Will," Mick Kinsella, who was dying, was persuaded to send for Andy Reynolds, a wizard at drawing up wills.

But before Andy could set down all the provisions, Mick died. That was a problem now for Andy because conscientious Nora Hallissey, the housekeeper, might testify at a legal contest that Mick died before he could attach his signature. Andy, to ease Nora's mind, trapped a live fly and thrust it quickly into the jaws of the deceased.

Then looking at Nora, Andy said, "And, if they put you in the (witness) box, remember that when he signed the will *there was life in him.*"

# CHAPTER 16

# Actions Speak Louder Than Laws

THE CITY CLERK in Jersey City, James Tumulty, will never be the same since a couple approached him in his office for a marriage license. In filling out the necessary form, Tumulty asked the couple, "Who'll perform the ceremony?"

The girl spoke up. "We just want the license."

"Yes, I know," Tumulty insisted, "but who'll marry you?"

Now it was the boy who answered. "We don't need nothin' but the license. We get ourselves married before we came in here."

The shadow of Montesquieu must have hovered over that office. In one of his many lucid moments the Frenchman stated that we should never try to create by law what can be accomplished by morality. But what are you going to do about unconventional people? The woods (and wards) are full of 'em. Take the case of the lady in Grand Rapids, Michigan. She reported to the police the loss of twenty dollars which she said was concealed in her stocking. The loss was discovered soon after the departure of a vacuum-cleaner salesman who had been demonstrating his line. Possibly her nature did not abhor a vacuum-cleaner salesman.

But don't feel too smug about such things. Maybe the law

hasn't yet caught up to your inhibited actions. Montaigne, another Frenchman, who convinced us that an epigram is a half-truth so stated as to irritate the person who believes the other half, implies that none of us is so good that, were we to submit all our thoughts and actions to the law, we would not deserve to be hung at least ten times in our lives. That is, unless you are Mrs. Goldie Sutton, of New Albany, Indiana.

Mrs. Sutton testified that her lately departed husband mistook her for *The Perils of Pauline*. He (1) threw her over a cliff, breaking her collar bone; he (2) doused her with kerosene and set her on fire; he (3) used her neck to demonstrate some rhumba steps; he (4) barely missed slashing her jugular vein with a razor; he (5) held a pan of hot grease over her head for interminable minutes; he (6) kicked her out of the window; and then he (7) singed her hair with a shotgun blast. The jury, convinced you can carry mayhem too far, acquitted the lady of first-degree murder.

Recently, in California, Justice Walter Derr fined artist Rodney Roth $50, ruling that the sound Valerie Humphries had made at a party when Roth bit her bare midriff was "a yell of pain" rather than, as the painter had testified, "a cry of ecstasy."

Crime marches on. In Brooklyn, Mosha Byron, reprimanded for shooting craps in his 100th year and arrested for illegally practicing medicine in his 102nd, was hauled into court again, this time for cursing a neighbor. He was ordered by a doubting judge to go home and get the birth certificate to prove his age as 108.

Last year in New Haven, Connecticut, a youth, chased by police to the roof of a nurses' dormitory, explained how he had happened to be lurking on the fire escapes outside the building: he "was looking for a men's room."

———•———

Myra Kingsley, the astrologer, noticed a sign on a Kentucky farmer's property:

### NOTIS

*Trespassers will be persecuted to the full*
*extent of two mongrel dogs which ain't never*
*been too sociable with strangers, and one*
*double barrel shotgun which ain't loaded with*
*sofa pillows.*
*Dam if I ain't gittin' tired of all this*
*fancy kedoodlin' in my lane.*

———•———

A Philadelphia magistrate demanded proof that a burlesque queen's dress was too flimsy. The proof: a detective folded the costume, squeezed it into a matchbox.

In the Bronx, Alan Siegel, summoned for smoking in a subway, defended himself in eight stanzas of wretched doggerel, got punishment to fit both crimes. The magistrate's decision: "Your poem is fine, it's quite a line. Next time heed 'No Smoking' sign. The verdict is $2 fine."

In Knoxville, Tennessee, the judge bound Neal Edwards to the grand jury for stealing a 100-lb. sack of flour, despite Edwards' contention that "somebody must have put it on my back . . ."

———•———

What's in a name? Here are some exhibits:

In Cleveland, May Dye got married and became May Linger. In the same city, Alexander Hamilton turned in Calvin Coolidge for passing a bum check.

An irate landlord in Trinidad sued David Cork for plugging the water tap. In Phoenix, Arizona, Wayne Flowers and Martha Trees asked for a marriage license, while in

Sydney, Australia, James Cain was charged with using indecent language to Police Constable Ronald Abel.

———— • • ————

A Chicago butcher, Louis Harris, finding that his Greek customers could not remember his name, went to court to have it changed back to Elias Haralampopoulos.

From Milwaukee comes the news that Kenneth Hanyzewski was sentenced to ninety days in jail for trying to forge Mike Grzadzieliwski's name to a check.

One of the legal name changes, arranged through proper courtroom channels, was that of Mike Stench.

He didn't like the name of Mike. So he had it legally changed to Joe Stench.

———— • • ————

Here are other name peculiarities:

In Paterson, New Jersey, Lillian Rentmeister was wed to Harry Fivehouse. Dorothy Snow of Omaha wisely chose lawyer Frank Frost to plead her divorce case.

In Luppitt, England, after fifty-nine years, Mary Stamp quit being postmistress. A man in Kansas, Robert Beer, was jugged for bootlegging.

———— • • ————

The teller at the bank in Brooklyn told Mary Considine that the check looked O.K., but in order to cash it she would have to endorse it.

"I don't understand," said Mary.

"What I want you to do," explained the teller, "is to sign your name just as you do on a letter."

"Oh, I see," said Mary, and, blushing, she wrote on the back of the check: "Lovingly yours, Mary Considine."

———— • • ————

Here's a chickadee who'll be a lady lawyer when she grows up. When she was only seven, she walked into a bank and asked to see the president. A smiling clerk showed her into his private office. She explained solemnly that her girls' club was raising money, and would he please contribute?

The banker laid a dollar bill and a dime on the desk and said, "You take whichever one you want."

She picked up the dime and said, "My mother always taught me to take the smallest piece," but picking up the dollar bill also, she added, "But so I won't lose this dime, I'll take this piece of paper to wrap it up in."

---

A great mind (Harpo Marx, if you're so insistent) once remarked that laws are like sausages. We have respect for them in so far as we know what they contain.

Some laws are so outlandish they must have been formulated by men who were undetected screwballs at the time. A Massachusetts law provides that no person shall travel on a sleigh drawn by a horse unless there are three bells attached. We wager the following year someone in that state introduced another bill making it a misdemeanor if the bells weren't tuned.

The Maine *Province and Court Record* for the year 1651 recorded a sentence imposed on a Miss Batcheller for adultery. The young lady was branded with the letter A.

The paper didn't state just where on her anatomy she was branded, but no matter where it was, we think that it is carrying matters too far.

Suppose this law had been on the New York statute books when a sailor entered the office of the ship's surgeon for a medical examination. The surgeon noticed that the sailor's chest was tattooed with the portraits of President Truman and Vice-President Barkley.

"My, but you're a patriot, aren't you?" commented the surgeon.

"You said it, Doc. You should see where I have Stalin and Malik."

Lyman E. Cook, St. Louis attorney, is a collector of freak laws. Here are some of his exhibits:

If you sing at a bar in Wisconsin, drive a red automobile in Minneapolis, eavesdrop in Oklahoma, marry your mother-in-law in the District of Columbia, or arrest a dead man for a debt in New York, you may run afoul of the law.

Legally, according to Cook, citizens of Barre, Vermont, are required to take a bath every Saturday night; every male in Brainerd, Minnesota, must grow a beard; and the female population of Providence, Rhode Island, cannot wear transparent apparel—even silk or nylon stockings.

Custom dictated many strange laws, yet when times changed no one remembered to repeal them. Thus, in Oregon a girl cannot legally enter an automobile with a young man unless accompanied by a chaperone. In Utah, daylight must be seen between a dancing couple. A man in Lewes, Delaware, cannot wear trousers that are form-fitting around the hips, while in Reading, Pennsylvania, a woman cannot hang underwear on a clothesline unless a screen is present.

Romance, of course, has always come under the law's scrutiny. Only a few years ago a husband was fined $15 for kissing his wife in a Chicago park. Kissing in public is also taboo in Georgia. In Massachusetts, a state surprisingly lenient with the tender passion, ten kisses are equivalent to a marriage proposal. A hug and kiss in the presence of the girl's parents, combined with several gifts of candy, are enough to announce your intentions in Minnesota; in Maryland, if you make six visits to a girl's home you are as good as hitched.

Once married, you can lawfully direct profanity at your wife if you live in Delaware, while in Michigan the law says a husband owns all his wife's clothing and can take possession of her entire wardrobe if she ever leaves him.

In matters of health, as well as heart, lawmakers have ruled sternly at times. A San Francisco ordinance prohibits the spraying of laundry clothes by water emitted from the mouth. Omaha bans the use of the same finger bowl by more than one person; and in Waterville, Maine, it is a violation to blow your nose in public. Indiana law declares that a mustache is "a known carrier of germs and a man cannot wear one if he habitually kisses human beings."

———•—•———

Asa G. Atwater tells the unusual story of a Pennsylvania farmer who was delinquent in payments on his new automobile. When the finance company official called, the farmer took him out to the barn where the car was set up on blocks, the wheels put away, and the automobile entirely protected by a cover. The car's mileage showed only the distance from showroom to farm. Just fifteen miles.

"The way I look at it," said the farmer, "is that the car isn't mine until it's paid for."

The finance company gladly extended the period of payment.

———•—•———

In Washington, D. C., a woman, who had bought her eleven-year-old daughter a war bond two years before, sent the Treasury a snapshot of the girl. Demanding the money that was promised on maturity, she explained: "You can see that she is very mature."

———•—•———

In Washington, Michael Prencipe, eighteen, prophesied to a *Times-Herald* inquiring photographer that 1949 "will be a good year for everyone." The next day he was arrested for house-breaking and bail-jumping by police who recognized his picture.

———•—•———

The City Commission of Salt Lake City ruled that, before City Judge Marcellus K. Snow could assume office, he would have to pay up his thirty-seven back parking fines.

Then there was the lawyer in Racine, Wisconsin, who kicked his client's shins three times in vain when the client started berating the judge. The lawyer found out later he had been kicking a wooden leg.

---

Andy Dutch thinks the only one who has the answer to life's exactions is the inmate of a California mental asylum he visited.

Andy asked him, "Why are you here?"

"Oh, I said the world was mad and they said I was mad . . ."

"You mean . . . ?"

"I was outvoted."

---

The librarian in Long Beach, California, had an unusual cause for New Year celebration: during the preceding year, she announced, no one had stolen a Bible from the city library.

---

Two other recent crime stories have a literary flavor.

When Little Rock police caught up with a youth who had broken into an automobile, they found he had also made off with a magazine called *Crime Does Not Pay*.

In Los Angeles, Mrs. Dorothy Hodel, a writer of children's books, drew ninety days for neglecting her children.

---

Jack Seaman vouches for this. The meek little man approached a policeman on the street corner.

"Excuse me, Officer," he said, "but I've been waiting here for my wife for over an hour. Would you be kind enough to order me to move on?"

---

Our politicos, too, have been running afoul of the law.

In South Miami, Florida, Julian Carballo was arrested for possessing bolita lottery tickets which he had brought to the city council meeting to show fellow council members that the gambling laws were not enforced.

In Indianapolis, a two-year prison sentence was given to Chester Allen Hunt, candidate for sheriff in the spring primaries, who had stumped Howard County in a stolen automobile.

———— • ————

Lanny Ross, the honey-toned warbler, asks a legal question. Can you answer it?

"Under the law of some states the attempt to commit a certain crime is punishable but the successful commission of the crime is never punishable. What crime is it?"

Do you have the answer yet? Suicide.

———— • ————

The Portuguese mayor of Estremadura it was who, in offering a reward for the recovery of the body of a drowned man, listed as a means of identification, that "the deceased had a marked impediment in his speech."

———— • ————

The police annals of Atlanta, Georgia, record this one. "What makes you say the prisoner was drunk, Officer?" asked the judge.

"He walked straight into a lamppost, was knocked down, arose and walked right into the lamppost. Backing off, he charged again and again. After four such contacts with the unyielding lamppost, the prisoner raised his head heavenward and exclaimed, 'Lost, lost, in an impenetrable forest.' "

———— • ————

Stephen Albright adds these gems to the collection, "Why People Behave Like Human Beings."

A policeman in Cambridge, Massachusetts, tore up a ticket for speeding after the clergyman he had stopped explained, "You have to be fast these days if you want to save souls."

Brought into court in Columbus, Ohio, on charges of

having destroyed a jukebox, William Oliver of that city told the judge that every time he inserted a nickel and tried to play *I Wonder What's Become of Sally,* the jukebox insisted on playing *Somebody Else Is Taking My Place.*

An automobile operated by a Camden, New Jersey, woman slid down an embankment and rested in the mud at the edge of a river. She sat there for nine hours and later told rescuers that although she could have climbed out she did not want to dirty her new shoes.

It's time the lawyers got together. Judge Blackstone says in his *Commentaries* that every bishop, parson, or vicar is a corporation. Lord Coke asserts in his reports (10 Rep. 32) that a corporation has no soul.

Upon these premises the logical inference would be that neither bishops, parsons, nor vicars have souls.

A man in Houston, arrested after being seen stuffing a small boy into the trunk of his car, confessed that he was hiding the child to save the price of one admission at a drive-in movie.

Albert French of Columbus, Ohio, complained that when he fell through the third-story window of a hotel and landed unhurt, the manager billed him for the broken glass.

Sidney Goldmann, prominent Jersey jurist, was State Librarian before he went on the bench.

A freshman law student came into the library and asked the location of a certain book. "It should be in those archives over there," said Goldmann.

The boy looked at him blankly. "In the what?"

"Archives. Don't you know what an archive is?"

Light hit the young man. "Oh, sure. That's where Noah kept his bees."

———•—•———

In Philadelphia, the City Hall reporters have always found a certain policeman "good copy."

Once as he was valiantly struggling to lift a drunk to his feet, a reporter asked him: "Who is he?"

"I don't know," replied the officer.

"Can't give an account of himself, eh?"

"Could you give an account," asked the cop, "if you lost your balance?"

Another occasion when the police had a dragnet on Roosevelt Boulevard and were stopping all cars, the same officer asked a New York autoist, "Do you have your driver's license with you?"

"Yes," answered the autoist. "Do you want to see it?"

"No," was the reply. "When you haven't got it with you is when I want to see it."

———•—•———

In Bristol, England, George Law recognized an automobile stolen from him three years before, despite fake engine and chassis numbers and a new paint job, and proved his ownership by pointing out a piece of chewing gum he had once used to patch an oil leak.

———•—•———

Charles Koktavy, of Milwaukee, arrested for printing football pool tickets, took a look at his warrant and announced proudly, "I printed these, too."

———•—•———

The FBI were tipped off that a long-haired gent sitting daily on a bench in Bryant Park, New York, was a subversive.

They brought him in for a checkup, along with a manuscript that was supposed to contain "treasonable evidence."

Within an hour they let him go because the chief told the operative, "This is a play in three acts. I've skimmed through it. I fail to see any plot."

------•--•------

On trial in Chile, Narciso Quezada and Violeta Munoz confessed that they had tied Violeta's husband to a table, tickled his feet until he choked to death with laughter.

------•--•------

There was a raid on a "bookie joint" in Boston. Among the indignant prisoners was a locksmith, who said: "I'm innocent, I tell you. I was making a bolt for the door when the cops broke in."

------•--•------

When the Earl of Bradford was questioned by the Lord Chancellor in a test of his sanity, he was asked, "How many 'egs has a sheep?"

"Does your lordship refer to a live sheep or a dead sheep?"

"It's the same thing," responded the Chancellor.

"Oh, no," insisted the earl. "A dead sheep has only two legs. The two forelegs are shoulders, and there are only two legs of mutton."

------•--•------

John L. Sullivan was hunted by New Jersey police for three years as the ringleader in a $2,000,000 holdup. He was caught trying to steal a $23 razor.

------•--•------

Sammy Epstein was a conscientious lawyer who was very careful about living up to every inch of the law. One day he came home and found his wife walking on the ceiling. "For goodness' sake," he demanded, "what do you think you're doing?"

"Walking on the ceiling," replied his wife, "and I'm having a wonderful time."

"You can't do that," protested Sammy. "It's breaking the law of gravity."

Immediately she fell to the floor with a bang. She sat stunned by the fall, then she burst into tears.

With a sob of resentment she cried to her husband: "Because you know the law, do you have to open your big mouth?"

———— • • ————

> Maud Muller, on a summer night,
> Turned down the only parlor light.
> The judge, beside her, whispered things
> Of wedding bells and diamond rings.
> He spoke his love in burning phrase,
> And acted foolish forty ways.
> When he had gone, Maud gave a laugh
> And then turned off the dictograph.

———— • • ————

In Indianapolis the city council has voted to sell a secluded, wooded spot on the north side purchased in the early '20s as a bird sanctuary. A councilman said he found most of the billing and cooing has been done in parked cars.

———— • • ————

In Akron, Ohio, when a man on trial for intoxication heard the officer testify the defendant's eyes were bloodshot, he defended himself by extracting a glass one and got probation.

———— • • ————

When Harold F. Ritz of Rochester, New York, climbed from his car to have words with the motorist who had bumped him, he found it was his wife.

———— • • ————

John L. Lewis occasionally makes the headlines. Not the least memorable of the exploits of the czar was the story carried in the San Antonio *Express* under the title: LEWIS WINS AND LOSES UNION SUIT.

———— • • ————

When a witness in the Dublin police court testified, "She conked me on the head and knocked me insensible," the

*Dublin Opinion,* with a bow to Oliver Goldsmith, came up with a prize headline:

### SHE CONKS TO STUPOR

The ingenuity of the criminal mind is demonstrated by a brace of recent news items.

An automobile dealer in McKeesport, Pennsylvania, complained to police that someone had stolen a new Lincoln right out of his display window.

A San Francisco jeweler, Harry Winters, reported that $950 had disappeared from his store while detectives were investigating a $45,000 burglary.

Then there was the lad in Superior, Wisconsin, who, pleading guilty to theft, explained that he thought the new price of $1 for a haircut must include the hair clippers.

The laurel, however, must be awarded to a man in Chicago. Held for larceny, he picked up a broom, swept busily past the guards, down the hall, and out the door of the county jail to freedom.

# CHAPTER 17

# Here Comes the Bribe

THE HUSBAND came home with some startling news.

"Honey," he said, "I'm going into politics."

"Honestly!" she exclaimed.

He sneered at her. "What difference does that make?"

This is the typical story that brands every politician as a guy who has got what it takes *to take what you got*. Or to paraphrase Gray's *Elegy*, politics is that place where "the paths of glory lead but to the gravy."

Our political leaders, for all the (gold) brickbats tossed at them, have the American grace for smiling in the face of such derogations. While some of them admit they spend half their time running for office and the other half running for cover, they also state in their own defense that in Greece, the very fountainhead of political thought, there was a bribe-taking Themistocles for every pure-living Socrates; a Pausanias committing perjury for every Plato who loved the truth.

The term politician has many connotations. There are many men in public life continually giving a competent account of their stewardship. Not in the city or town where you are now reading this . . . but elsewhere. There are conscientious legislators giving freely of their time, energy, and devotion to the public weal. Not in your state, however. Where you reside there isn't a legislator who would turn any wheel unless it was well greased. Yes, there are many honest men in government. One of these days they are going to be exposed. And those who have been saying that politics is a game, where you either pass the buck or the doe, will apologize. While this is the Age of Chiselry you will still find in the Town Hall, the courthouse or the State House many conscientious public servants. They are constantly fighting a governmental system that is supposed to be one of checks and balances. But few politicians take a check and seldom do they leave a balance.

What is the line of demarcation between those who work gratis and those who work gratuities?

Merely the conscientious, individual desire to serve the community or himself. Many political workers are content with their jobs. Or to paraphrase Hugo Sonnenschein, Jr.:

> All types of politicos you meet,
> They work for state and county,
> To get such jobs is quite a feat—
> There's no mutiny on the public bounty.

Editor Herb Saal had to correct his youthful reporter. "Never say that every member of the Fourth Ward Political Club takes graft."

"But they all do."

"Yes, I know," said the editor, "but let's avoid trouble. Say that every member of the club, with one exception, takes graft. Then no member of the club will feel personally offended."

A politician's popularity rises during that period when he raises the most pleasing issues and promises every voter exactly what is nearest to the voter's heart. The storm breaks when the notes come due and go to protest. For the most unsecured paper in the world is the election pledge.

Most politicians defend this procedure by saying that the

proper way to catch a fish is never to throw a straight shadow over the water. A crooked shadow is mistaken for an overhanging bough. Thus are issues presented to the voter.

Bob Hope said he didn't know what the issues were in an election in Wilkes-Barre. He didn't even know there was an election. He was driving through the city and put his hand out to signal a left turn. Immediately, eight candidates shook it.

———•—•———

During a spirited campaign for sheriff, one of the candidates was spouting off, according to Tom Nugent.

Two of the electorate were listening. "Who is he?" asked one.

"I don't know," said the other, "but he is sure recommending himself."

———•—•———

Another candidate who knew neither geography nor Greek once bellowed that his principles would prevail "from Alpha to Omaha."

———•—•———

During World War II, the draft board in one of our eastern cities was visited by one of the local city commissioners, a man of limited education. In fact, he would have to take off his shoes and socks to count up to twenty.

The commissioner addressed the chairman of the board. "Mac," he said, "this lady here is Mrs. Raskowski, and this is her son, Stanley. You sent Stanley word to report here, but the boy is nuts. And how do I know he hasn't got all his buttons? His old lady says so and if your mother says you're bugs, you must be."

The chairman spoke. "I'm sure, Commissioner, the Army is not anxious to take any mental cases. However, for the record, I would like the boy to take the witness stand that I might test him with a few questions."

The boy was brought forward. The chairman pointed a serious finger at him. "Tell me. Who cut down the cherry tree?"

The boy cringed in his chair. "Honest, mister, I didn't do it."

The commissioner jumped up. "Look, Mac," he said, "I've known this kid since he was that high. Now if he says he didn't do it, you can believe him."

The chairman of the draft board concealed his smile, but the commissioner detected an attitude of unbelief. "Look, Mac," he said, as he drew out a roll of bills, "what's the sense of quibbling? How much are the damages to the cherry tree? We'll pay for it right now."

———•—•———

A U. S. senator once refused to be drawn into a controversy with an insignificant opponent. He explained his attitude in this way, "A skunk once challenged a lion to a fight. In declining, the lion said, 'You would gain fame fighting a lion while everyone who met me for a month would know I was in the company of a skunk.'"

———•—•———

Calvin Coolidge, when he practiced law, was once consulted by a political leader who wanted to sue an opponent for slander.

"Don't do it," advised Coolidge.

"Why not?"

"Because," said Cal with Yankee sagacity, "one should never engage in a micturition contest with a skunk."

———•—•———

Political fights will always be with us. It's a part of the great game. Once a Democratic congressman, thoroughly enraged, told a Republican colleague "to go to hell."

"Thanks," said the Republican. "That's the first time I was ever invited to Democratic headquarters."

Stanley Walker, ace newspaperman, was listening to a political rally in a small town in New Mexico. The candidate was really pouring it on.

He bellowed, he cajoled, he waved his arms, he performed acrobatics, all in the process of selling himself to the electorate.

Stanley asked an old Mexican, "Who is that?"

The answer had the rock-ribbed philosophy of Spanish culture. "Es un hombre de muchas pulgas." (He's a man with many fleas.)

———•———

Some years ago, Hattie Caraway, the shy little lady senator from Arkansas, stepped to the front of the platform to be introduced to one of the last home audiences she would meet before she returned to Washington.

The man who introduced her was very enthusiastic about her accomplishments and reviewed her record in glowing terms. He was shouting when he reached the climax.

"Ladies and gentlemen, we'll now hear from the most notorious woman in Arkansas."

———•———

He was defeated for sheriff, receiving only fifty-five votes out of a total of 3,500. Next day he walked down Main Street with two guns hanging from his belt.

"You were not elected and you have no right to carry guns," fellow citizens told him.

"Listen, folks," he replied, "a man with no more friends than I've got in this county needs to carry guns."

———•———

The City Council of Los Angeles had a proposed ordinance to be voted on. It would require dogs, chickens, cats, turkeys, canaries, and donkeys to be silent in the city between 10 P.M. and 6 A.M.

Councilman Byron Brainerd was deeply worried. "I'd like

to vote for this ordinance. But can dogs read? How will they know when they should not bark?"

———— • • ————

The President was awakened by his wife, who said: "Call someone, there are burglars in the house."

"No, my dear," he said. "Maybe in the Senate, but not in the House."

———— • • ————

The penitent was in the confessional box. "Bless me, Father, for I have sinned," he whispered to the priest. "Some time ago I killed two Republican election workers—"

The priest interrupted him. "I'm not interested in your politics, only in your sins."

———— • • ————

Sam Parish recalls the successful mayoralty candidate who was approached by one of his campaign workers.

"I have a son," said the constituent, "who needs a job. Can I count on your help?"

"Sure," said the politico, "what does he do?"

"Frankly," replied the man, "nothing."

"Good!" said the mayor-elect. "Then we won't have to break him in!"

———— • • ————

It was a meeting of the Lithuanian-American Democratic Club and the boss had come over to speak. He ripped and roared at the opposition; he harangued and he hollered about Republican corruption. But when he sat down, there was nary a handclap.

Then the chairman of the meeting arose and spoke in the native tongue. The Liths were now in feverish excitement. They followed every gesture and at the end of the speech they stood up and cheered heartily.

The boss turned to the chairman. "What line did you feed em that makes 'em jump?"

"Boss," said the henchman, "all I did was repeat *your* speech in our lingo."

———•·•———

There is a pronounced rift between a certain state commissioner and his secretary.

He dictated a memo for the budget director, setting forth the duties of a new male assistant and thereby justifying his presence on the payroll. When the memo was typed and returned to him for correction, the commissioner nearly swooned. He hopes he has destroyed all copies.

The memo read: The principal activities of this senior clerk is to take care of some of the *cuties* of the commissioner.

———•·•———

The late Governor Folk of Missouri, accompanied by a friend, arrived at his office one morning to find a number of men waiting for him in the anteroom. He paused as he passed through and told a very ancient joke. In his office, the friend said, "That was an awfully old chestnut you pulled out there."

"I know it," the governor replied, "but I wanted to find out how many of those fellows were here to ask favors."

"And did you?"

"Oh, yes," said Folk. "They were the ones who laughed."

———•·•———

With our experiences during the Prohibition experiment, with all the theories of various crime commissions inundating the daily papers, we believe the only common-sense attitude on racketeering came from an obscure sheriff.

He said, "The only way we can stop gambling and killing in this country is to pass laws legalizing 'em."

———•·•———

In the recent Newark City Commission campaign, there was a heated argument in one of the ward clubs. Two men were tearing into each other in a quarrel over some phase of strategy.

"Oh, you're crazy!" shouted one.

"No, I'm not crazy," denied the other.

"But you *are* crazy!" repeated the first.

"I can prove that I am not crazy, and that's more than *you* can do," came back the challenge.

"Let's see you prove it, then."

Thereupon the man accused of being crazy pulled from an inside pocket his discharge papers from a nearby insane asylum.

———•———

He was applying for county relief and the young lady official was filling out the customary form. "Do you owe any back house rent?" she asked.

"We ain't had no backhouse for years," he replied with great dignity. "We got modern plumbing."

———•———

Elizabeth Fowler Draper knows the breed.

> His campaign was a pleasant one,
> And worthy here of note;
> He only kissed the babies who
> Were old enough to vote.

———•———

There is a North Jersey freeholder whose vermilion complexion is even redder since he attended a dinner recently.

A monsignor, beloved by his parishioners, was being honored on the twenty-fifth anniversary of his pastorate. Our freeholder was chairman of the affair, but he had been delayed in reaching the hotel where the dinner was served. The toastmaster proceeded without him.

After all the laudations had been heaped upon the venerable monsignor, he rose to their tribute. "The seal of the confessional," he said, "can never be broken and so I can only hint gently of my impressions when I came here to you twenty-five years ago. Oh, I thought I had wandered into a horrible place. The first chap who entered the confessional box told me a hair-raising tale of stealing a suit of clothes and, when halted by an officer, almost murdering the policeman. But as the days went on I knew I had entered a land of fine, lovely people."

When the monsignor finished, there was some excitement at the door. The freeholder had arrived. He was rushed to the dais to make the gift presentation speech.

Beaming on them all, the freeholder spoke. "I'll never forget the first day our monsignor arrived in this parish. In fact, I have the honor of being the first one to go to him in confession."

———————

They resorted to everything, even bribery, before they got Joe Marsh into the local fire department. He had failed so many civil service tests that finally, in desperation, they asked him to draw a horse. At that, he left off one of the ears and they could only give him 98%.

One of the questions he had answered was this. "A pyromaniac? That's a guy who goes nuts from eating too many pies."

———————

As soon as the ladies were given the constitutional privilege of voting, the Republican party marshalled some of its forceful and well-groomed women. They were sent into women's clubs to preach the good Republican doctrine, explain the fundamentals of political science, etc.

One chic speaker addressed the then new League of Women Voters, stressing the need for an awakened and intelligent response by women to this new responsibility.

"And, now," she smiled sweetly on them, "I'd be glad to answer any questions."

A hand rose in the rear. "Yes?"

"Tell me," asked the questioner, "how do you get that smooth effect about the hips?"

---

Once when Henry Clay failed to recognize a young lady, she said reproachfully, "Why, Mr. Clay, you don't remember my name!"

"No," answered the statesman in his most gallant manner, "for when we last met I was sure your beauty and accomplishments would soon compel you to change it."

---

He is a bureau chief in a state highway department and his official O.K. can clear a voucher for payment.

The contractor sauntered in. "Lovely day," he said. His hand drew from his pocket a $100 bill, which he nonchalantly tossed toward the Bureau Chief.

"Have a cigar?" asked the B.C.

"Thanks." The contractor sniffed the cigar and slapped it into the wise-guy angle of his mouth. The Bureau Chief's pocket lighter came into view. He ignited the $100 bill and blazed it across the table until it lighted the contractor's cigar. Then coolly he held the burning bill against his own cigar. The charred remains fell into the waste basket.

Neither of the men spoke. It was not necessary.

---

In the French parliament, one of the deputies, making a speech urging the improvement of the legal status of women, cried: "After all, there is very little difference between men and women!"

With one accord, the entire Chamber of Deputies rose and shouted, *"Vive la différence!"*

---

The editor had to reprove the new city hall reporter. "While I like this sentence, 'One usually gets only fallen arches out of uplift movements,' I must correct your final assumption."

"What did I write that's wrong?"

"The reform party nominates for mayor the owner of our largest brewery and selects for its candidate for district attorney the president of the local Temperance League."

"That's just what they did, Chief. They picked Chet Lambert and Mildred Audenbach."

"I don't dispute that. It's the headline you suggest. Do you want us to have a libel suit?"

"What did I say?"

"Politics Makes Strange Bedfellows."

---

Maybe there are only two political groups, the appointed and the disappointed, but one glaring headline in the daily paper aroused the city hall. It read:

HALF THE CITY COUNCIL ARE CROOKS.

A retraction in full was demanded of the editor under threat of a libel suit. Next afternoon the headline read:

HALF THE CITY COUNCIL AREN'T CROOKS.

---

The councilmen probably agreed with Paul Morris:

> Ah, me! 'Tis the penalty I must endure:
> Yes, fame incites gossip. I'll sue!
> You see, of the stories they tell about me,
> Half of the lies are not true!

---

One of old Tom Pendergast's henchmen called Democratic headquarters in Kansas City one election day. He was positively peeved.

"Send some reinforcements over to my ward right away,"

he said. "There's a bunch of guys voting as they damn please."

———•——•———

A certain U. S. senator, noted for his pomposity, was once sounding off before Dorothy Parker. "It's one of the disadvantages of statesmanship," he said, "to realize, as Heraclitus did, that there'll always be a majority of fools. I simply can't bear fools."

"How paradoxical," said Dorothy. "Your mother could."

———•——•———

Two angry candidates of opposing political beliefs rushed at each other. Friends stepped in to separate them. Each struggled to get at the other. The first, seeing the extremely violent efforts of his opponent, exclaimed: "More of you men hold Jones! One man can hold me!"

———•——•———

In Frankfort, Kentucky, after state legislators fell to wrestling and brandishing pistols during a heated floor debate, Democratic Representative M. G. Thompson, a licensed gun dealer, admitted selling "about a dozen" items of small arms to this year's incumbents.

———•——•———

Former Senator Bill Hunt, publisher of the Wildwood (N.J.) *Leader,* one day noticed on the rack a "filler" item . . . As we approached the apiary, there was a cluster of bees evidently fighting among themselves.

He reached for his pencil and chuckled, "Here's the proper headline for that item." And he wrote: CASE OF THE HIVES VERSUS THE HIVE-NOTS.

———•——•———

Some time ago a woman presented herself at a registration booth with the intention of enrolling and casting her first vote in the coming election. She gave her name, her address, and her age, and then the clerk of registration asked her this question: "What party do you affiliate with?"

The woman's eyes popped. "Do I have to answer that question?" she demanded.

"That is the law," he told her.

"Then you jes' scratch my name off the books," she said. "If I gotta tell his name I don' wanna vote. Why, he ain't got his divorce yet." And she stalked out.

———•••———

From the trade journal *Tobacco:*

"It has been fifteen years since Tipton, California, has had a mayor who smoked. Mayor North never smoked, ex-Mayor Calman doesn't smoke, and Mayor Chapman never smoked when living."

# CHAPTER 18

# Deep in the Heart of Taxes

MOST POLITICAL REVOLUTIONS are born in the first tax bill. Years ago in one of the Bungle cartoons, George was going into politics until business picked up. All of us have had a tax hangover since the Boston Tea Party.

The townspeople of Hanover, New Hampshire, once levied a poll tax on Dartmouth students. The college boys ganged up on the townspeople at the next meeting. Outnumbering the local voters, the students set up ordinances and voted for their passage whereby Hanover would have to build a town hall an inch square and a mile high; construct a sidewalk with a canopy over it leading to Colby Junior College, a girls' school forty miles away.

The following year the students voted a law for a subway to Smith College and an eight-lane concrete highway to Skidmore, like Smith a college for women. The town of Hanover desperately appealed to the state legislature to annul these laws and the students thereafter went untaxed.

Again, there were those Rensselaer Polytechnic undergraduates who quietly cornered all the pennies in town— 250,000 in all, collected from banks and stores. The students claimed the pennies represented "hidden taxes" levied by the government. Business was hampered for several days, with not a penny to be had.

Suddenly hundreds of students descended upon the stores

and began making purchases with copper coins. For at least a week merchants in Rensselaer and nearby Troy were acutely conscious of "hidden taxes" by seeing them piled in mountainous stacks around their cash registers.

This reminds us of the friend who said to a theater owner, "Why are you placing those sharp-pointed objects on all the seats?"

The theater owner smiled. "I want the people to become tacks conscious."

———————

In one congressional district the taxpayers decided to dine their representative so that, in a convivial atmosphere, they could discuss their tax problems.

One of the garrulous damsels monopolized the congressman's time. He restrained his annoyance.

"You should be balancing the budget," she said shrilly. "What are you waiting for?"

"Madam, just a chance to eat this chicken."

———————

When an old South African native was told he had to be taxed because the government, like a father, protected him from enemies, cared for him when he was sick, fed him when he was hungry, gave him an education, and for these purposes needed money, the old native said:

"Yes, I understand. It is like this: I have a dog and the dog is hungry. He comes to me and begs food.

"I say to him: 'My dear faithful dog, I see you are very hungry. I am sorry for you. I shall give you meat.'

"I then take a knife, cut off the dog's tail, give it to him, and say, 'Here, my faithful dog, be nourished by this nice piece of meat.'"

How much nourishment could be given to instructors at agricultural colleges posed a tax problem in Massachusetts. There had been a proposal before the state legislature to raise faculty salaries. As Mrs. R. H. of North Amherst describes it, the farm bloc was solidly against the measure—they couldn't see why the state should pay those college professors $5,000 a year just for talking twelve or fifteen hours a week. Faculty representatives made no headway with their arguments until one of them, who had had some farming experience, had an inspiration.

"Gentlemen," he told the lawmakers, "a college professor is a little like a bull. It's not the amount of time he spends. It's the importance of what he does!"

The professors got their raise.

Bernardine Kielty, in her always interesting *Book-of-the-Month Club News*, gives the taxpayers a whimsical glimpse of life in Washington. She attributes the story to George Gallup.

A congressman was chiding the Department of Agriculture for its free and easy way with the taxpayers' money. Look at the stuff it printed, said he, hundreds of pamphlets in which no one had the slightest interest—*The Recreational Resources of the Denison Dam, The Wolves of Mount Mc-Kinley, The Ecology of the Coyote*. "They print every last thing about Nature but the love life of the frog."

Shortly after his harangue, the Department of Agriculture was surprised to find in the mail five or six letters from congressmen asking for *The Love Life of the Frog*. Similar orders kept coming in so regularly that the Department was obliged to state in a circular, "We do *not* print *The Love Life of the Frog*." After the public announcement was made, requests for *The Love Life* were trebled. It got to be such a headache that the Department finally issued a press release stating that it had never printed a pamphlet about the love life of the frog, and wanted to hear no more about the whole thing.

When this news item came out in the papers, requests began to climb into the hundreds. By now the matter had got out of hand and the Secretary of Agriculture himself was called in. Determined to stop the foolishness once and for all, he took time during an address on the air, on a nation-wide hookup, to deny vehemently that the Department had ever prepared any pamphlet concerning the love life of the frog, that to his knowledge there never was such a pamphlet, and that even if there had been the Department wouldn't have printed it. After the broadcast there were more than a thousand requests in the mail.

———•—•———

High taxes are accompanied by high rents. So one tenement house inspector found a group solution to the rent problem. There were four families living in one room, chalk lines being drawn across the floor to mark off a quarter for each family.

"How have you been getting along here?" inquired the inspector.

"Very well," was the reply, "until the lady in the far corner began to take in boarders."

———•—•———

If there was another president of the United States as frugal as Cal Coolidge, who was it? Cal always had economy on his mind.

While in office, he decided to visit Chicago. To the despair of the Secret Service men, Cal insisted on a regularly scheduled train, rather than an expensive special. The President and Mrs. Coolidge occupied the unpretentious Pullman drawing room. Mr. Coolidge even went into the diner for his breakfast. The dining car steward hovered over him to see that the service was flawless, and at the breakfast's end the steward beamed, "Was the coffee all right, Mr. President?"

"Why?" drawled Calvin. "Was anything supposed to be the matter with it?"

———•—•———

Cal was always a "stand-up guy." When Rupert Hughes wrote his uninhibited *Life of George Washington,* revealing George as a gent who could handle both a goblet and a girl, the Washington newspapermen piled into the White House.

"Our editors think, Mr. President, that you should resent these aspersions on George Washington's memory. Will you say something?"

President Coolidge walked to the window and parted the curtains. "I see his monument is still standing."

———•—•———

One irate taxpayer rushed into the City Hall in Jersey City and pointed his index finger under the nose of Deputy Mayor John Malone. "I want you to know there's a political renaissance coming."

Malone sneered. "He can't see Mayor Hague without an appointment."

———•—•———

Senator James Hamilton Lewis of Illinois was one legislator who was free of the common illusions. He was wont to tell new members of the Senate:

"You must not feel too humble. You see, you spend your first six months wondering how you got into the Senate. After that, you wonder how the other members got there."

———•—•———

Felix Tumulty, brother of Woodrow Wilson's secretary, was pleading from the platform one night in favor of the movement to reduce taxes.

A drunken heckler annoyed him. "I know you, Tumulty, you're a demagogue."

"And I know you," retorted Felix, "you're a demijohn."

*"You must not feel too humble. You see, you spend your first six months wondering how you got into the Senate. After that, you wonder how the other members got there."*

It must be traditional to torment the tumultuous Tumultys, but it never does a heckler any good.

Felix's nephew, Assemblyman T. James Tumulty, is a hefty person, hitting the scales at around two hundred and fifty pounds. At a tax meeting in the City Hall of Jersey City, the assemblyman was attacked by a woman who should have known that a fertile mind lay behind that avoirdupois.

"Don't pay any attention to Tumulty," she snarled. "I once dropped him on his head when he was a baby."

Cherubic Jim smiled disarmingly. "I'll bet you couldn't do it now," he said.

Such a glib retort was equalled only by a remark dropped in the British Parliament.

Addison was making his first speech. A gifted writer, he now stumbled for words out of sheer nervousness. He stammered, "Mis . . . Mis . . . Mister . . . Speake . . . Speaker, I con . . . con . . . conceive. I con . . . con . . . ceive . . . I con . . . con . . . conceive . . ."

He was interrupted by a voice from the gallery. "Why don't you sit down? You've conceived three times and brought forth nothing."

————◆◆————

When the Case Legislative Commission visited Hudson County, New Jersey, in 1928, to inquire into corruption and high taxes, Senator Clarence Case was interrupted during his piercing revelations of the Hague political machine.

Supervisor John O'Neill constantly cut in with statements attesting to the efficiency of subordinate employees.

Senator Case whirled on O'Neill. "When we're disposing of the dog, why worry about the fleas on his back?"

————◆◆————

Hugh Newton contributes this bit of Washington lore: The metal strips used to band birds are inscribed: "Notify Fish and Wild Life Service, Washington, D. C." They used to read "Notify Washington Biological Survey," abbreviated to "Wash. Biol. Surv." This was changed after a farmer shot a crow and then disgustedly wrote the U. S. Government:

"Dear Sirs: I shot one of your pet crows the other day and followed instructions attached to it. I washed it and biled it and surved it. It was turrible. You should stop trying to fool the people with things like this . . ."

The fireside audience who heard F.D.R.'s reiterative phrase, "again and again and again," may have pondered its origin. It appears in a limerick quoted by Osbert Sitwell as a favorite of John Sargent, the noted artist.

> There was a young lady of Spain,
> Who often got sick on a train,
>    Not once and again,
>    But again and again,
> And again and again and again.

America had no greater exponent of liberty than Patrick Henry. In his day our liberty was associated with the doctrine of taxation and no representation. This story has to do with a man who loved to deliver in public an oration on Patrick Henry. He spoke so often that everyone had heard his speech several times and all were heartily tired of it.

Deciding to cure him for once and for all, they arranged for a meeting with a group of farmers from the area. The night before the meeting they went to the local man and told him that at the last minute their speaker from the Agricultural College had been unable to come and asked if he would take his place. As always, the local speaker was happy to oblige.

"However," the committee spokesman continued, "there is just one hitch. We have invited the farmers in to hear a talk on a certain subject and they are coming for that, so you must speak on that subject lest they be disappointed."

The speaker said that he would do so and asked the subject. The topic, said the committee, was "Colic In Mules." The local speaker said he would do the best he could.

The next night everyone was at the meeting to hear what he would say. After announcing the subject, "Colic In Mules," he began:

"Colic in mules is caused by gas in the alimentary canal of the mule, which rushes back and forth, saying, 'Give me liberty or give me death.'"

———•———

When, on the death of President McKinley, Theodore Roosevelt succeeded to the highest office, a New York editor desired to contrast the event with a recent coronation in Europe. But—the compositor, coming to the word "oath" in the manuscript, struck a wrong key and the sentence appeared, "For sheer democratic dignity, nothing could exceed the moment when, surrounded by the cabinet, Mr. Roosevelt took a simple bath as President of the United States."

———•———

Paradoxically, a great friendship existed between Teddy Roosevelt, the Republican, and "Big Tim" Sullivan, Democratic leader of Tammany Hall. Whenever Big Tim was in Washington he was always a welcome visitor at the White House.

On one such occasion, Tim spoke to the President in behalf of a constituent, "I'd like you to help this young man, Mr. President. He's in a little trouble."

"Such as?"

"Oh, something trivial. They caught him robbing the mails in the New York Post Office and they sent him to Leavenworth."

The President promised to look into the case. After several months a probationary report was placed on Teddy's desk and within weeks he signed a pardon for the young man. Big Tim was elated.

A year passed. Then Teddy casually asked Sullivan, "Tim, I've often thought of that young man we pardoned. What has become of him?"

"Mr. President," said Tim, "you'll never regret what you did for that boy. Your actions restored him to society."

"What's he doing now?" asked Teddy.

"He's running a wheel at Canfield's," said Tim, Canfield's being New York's most notorious gambling casino.

---

Issues are to be seen, heard, and then promptly forgotten. Even if you remembered on what issue your candidate was elected, it is ten to one he has forgotten it the morning after election.

But if events are entrusted to Mr. Judd of Florida, we may see a new phase of political conduct. A member of a Kiwanis Club, Mr. Judd, has proposed the organization of an SFCP Society . . . "Society for Fulfillment of Campaign Promises."

Under Mr. Judd's plan, as outlined to Kiwanians, clubs would be organized in each city to check politicians after elections "to see that they deliver the goods we voted for." Mr. Judd suggested public ducking for all candidates who failed to live up to their campaign promises after the elections.

---

At a state banquet given by Frederick the Great of Prussia to his courtiers and nobles, the monarch asked those present to explain why his revenues continued to diminish despite incoming taxes. An old general of the hussars remarked dryly, "I will show your majesty what happens to the money."

Procuring a piece of ice, he lifted it high for inspection,

then handed it to his neighbor and requested that it be passed on from hand to hand to the king. By the time it reached Frederick, it was about the size of a pea.

----•--•----

Or as Brother Edgerton phrased it:

> There are candidates in front of us,
> And candidates to rear,
> All promising the universe
> In presidential year.
> But when they take their offices,
> And brooms with which to sweep,
> We wonder just how many of
> Their promises they'll keep.

----•--•----

Into the Camden tax office came a man who had, within the week, been in a slight motor accident. Adhesive tape crossed the bridge of his nose.

Being there to pay his taxes, he drew out a roll of bills and passed them across the collector's cage.

"Had an accident to your nose?" The collector was urbane, deferential.

"No," said John Citizen, "I've been paying through it so long it's given away under the strain."

----•--•----

Councilman Jim Segriff tells of the outraged tenant in Long Beach, New York, who, during the bureaucratic days of O.P.A., wrote the local price administrator:

"I hear you are in charge of ceilings. The tenant above me weighs four hundred pounds and my ceiling is beginning to crack. Do something."

----•--•----

Another bureaucrat, this time from an agricultural office, saw a Texas farmer dumping raw vegetables into the hog trough.

"Don't you know," said the bureaucrat, "that if you

cooked those vegetables, the hogs could digest them in half the time?"

"What's that?" replied the farmer, momentarily interested.

Then, after taking time to consider the import of the other's remark, he added, "Suppose they could! What in heaven's name is time to a hog?"

———•———

An irate taxpayer in Boston sent his check in, addressed to:

CITY HAUL

BOSTON, MASS.

———•———

In Salt Lake City, the city commissioners paid a firm of experts $2,500 to recommend improvements in the city government. The experts recommended that the commissioners' jobs be abolished.

———•———

"Organization," in the words of C. R. House, "is the art of getting men to respond like thoroughbreds.

"When you cluck to a thoroughbred, he gives you all of the speed and strength of heart and sinew in him. If you cluck to a jackass, he kicks."

But for the true definition of political organization, how about this factual story?

Into the law offices of George Cutley one day there thundered an excitable chap. "George," he said, "we will have to do something about Mickey O'Neill."

"What's the matter with Mickey O'Neill?" asked Mr. Cutley.

"Matter? They's plenty the matter. They's a guy runnin' aroun' wid Mickey's wife!"

"Is that my concern?"

"George, you don' understand. Mickey knows about it, and he won't do anything about it!"

"Well, if Mickey won't do anything about it, why should we?"

The excitable chap shook his head sadly. "George, you *still* don' understand. We've got to do somethin'. This guy what's runnin' aroun' wid Mickey's wife ain't even a member of the organization."

———•·•———

In Des Moines, an astute state representative, Harold Nelson, left a cigar box planted with corn sprouts atop his desk, feeling confident that restless farmer-legislators would demand adjournment when the sprouts began to sprout.

———•·•———

Giovanni Villa of Palermo, Sicily, who has spent four years trying to get himself declared officially alive, complained that the only person convinced thus far is the tax collector.

———•·•———

Dr. S. Weir Mitchell, Philadelphia's famed physician and novelist (*Hugh Wynne, Free Quaker*), once took umbrage at a visitor who called the Philadelphia City Hall a "vision of beauty."

"It is not that," punned Dr. Mitchell, "rather call it a division of booty."

———•·•———

They were discussing a certain undefeatable and irrepressible politician.

"Well," summed up the smokeroom philosopher, "I'll tell you this about him. He might have typhoid, and recover; he might have pneumonia, and recover; he might have cerebral meningitis, and recover; he might have yellow fever, and recover; but—if he ever had lockjaw, by gad, sir, he'd burst!"

———•·•———

Barbara C. McNamee reports this. Near a big government building, a Washington bureaucrat parked his car in a lot with a sign which read: "All day parking 35 cents." At lunchtime he asked the boy at the gate if he could drive his car to his luncheon appointment and bring it back after an hour without having to pay a second time.

The attendant's reply was wholly Washingtonian: "Suh, each car comes in has to pay 35 cents, and don' argue with me. I'se not on the policy-making level."

---

Perhaps no one has enjoyed the gentle ribbing about her peregrinations more than the gracious lady who stood loyally and affectionately by the side of F.D.R. Here is a Leonard Lyons version.

A father was telling his young son the tale of Robinson Crusoe. "And one day he saw strange footprints in the sand," the father recited. "He was puzzled. For they weren't his footprints. He hadn't seen anybody else on the island. And this island was far, far away from all other lands. And he said to himself, 'Whose footprints could these be?'" The youngster put in, "I know. Eleanor Roosevelt's."

---

Over the door of the log cabin retreat of the superintendent of schools of Phillips, Wisconsin, appears the legend:

BORED OF EDUCATION.

---

In Litchfield, Minnesota, the county treasurer pondered the note pinned to an irate citizen's tax return: "The cannibals had a way of solving high taxes . . . they ate the tax collector."

---

David Forrest of Burbank, California, reports an interesting brush with Marxism:

To help me in mastering Russian, I was eager to buy records of Russian folk songs to learn by ear. I finally located a tiny establishment with a wonderful store of records, sheet music, and booklets to brighten the way of the traveler to

Russia. The proprietor, a stern little man, beamed when he heard of my plan. "I am fifteen years Paris. I am eight years South America. I am six years this country. But I am born in Russia. Never in my life have I seen such a country. You are smart. You study. You go there. Wonderful! What a country!"

"And you are anxious to return?" I asked.

The man was silent a moment before replying. Then he said, "Trouble with me is, I am *crazy* about your rotten capitaleestic seestem."

Nate Collier suggests this motto for a politician:

MERRILY WE ROLL A LOG.

Reporting a cruiser's launching at Newport News, Virginia, the Superior (Wisconsin) *Telegram* said: "Taking the bottle of champagne in both hands and swigging it like a veteran, Mrs. Hatch started the *Duluth* on its journey auspiciously."

Thomas R. Marshall, Vice-President under Wilson, was a great admirer of the President. One of the books Marshall wrote was dedicated: "To President Woodrow Wilson from his only Vice."

Public officials hate controls over rent, food, and other commodities. There is always too much "red tape." Filling out forms and ration cards induces trouble. Also laughs, as the following communications attest. They came into the office of a Milk Control Board in England.

(1) Please send me a form for cheap milk as I am expecting mother.

(2) Please send me a form for supply of milk for having children at reduced prices.

(3) I posted the form by mistake before my child was filled in properly.

(4) I have a baby eighteen months old—thank you for the same.

(5) Will you please send me a form for cheap milk? I have a baby two months old and did not know anything about it till a friend told me.

(6) I had intended coming to the Milk Office today, but had fifteen children this morning.

(7) I have a child nearly two years old and looking forward to an increase in November. Hoping this will suit your kind approval.

(8) I have a baby two years old fed entirely on cows and another four months old.

(9) Will I be able to have milk for baby as my husband finishes his job as night watchman on Thursday?

(10) Sorry I have been so long filling in my form, but I have been in bed for two weeks with my baby and did not know it was running out till the milkman told me.

———•—•———

Mr. T. B. Akoury lives in a house which straddles two states, New York and Vermont, and you can take his word for it, his situation is a taxpayer's nightmare.

The house, built in 1783, is partly in New York and partly in Vermont. But that's only the beginning. The house stands in three counties—Washington and Rensselaer in New York, and Bennington County in Vermont. And that's still not all.

The house was built within the corporate limits of four towns—Hoosick and White Creek, New York, and Bennington and Shaftsbury, Vermont.

The owner, Mr. Akoury, pays taxes to two states, three counties, and four towns—which must be some sort of record in taxpaying.

Florence Southard knows a tax-resisting, unreconstructed rebel in New England. He is ninety-nine years old.

"I guess you've seen some changes in your day," someone said to him.

"Yep," he snapped back, "and I've been agin every one of 'em."

———•·•———

When an American importer approached Twining, the famous London tea merchants, to negotiate for the American distribution rights for their brand, an elderly Twining was not too friendly about it. He harrumphed and said, "You know, we had quite a lot of trouble over there."

"Trouble?" asked the importer.

"Yes," said Mr. Twining, "they dumped a shipment of our tea into Boston Harbor."

———•·•———

In Middletown, New York, a patriotic citizen, after drinking two quarts of blackberry wine and a half a quart of gin every week to help ease the water shortage, complained bitterly that the State Tax Bureau had rejected the deduction on his income tax return.

———•·•———

H. G. Wells had such a big head that he had trouble getting hats to fit. Once when he found one that balanced nicely on his head he just walked off with it, and blandly penned a note to its owner, E. S. Peck, mayor of Cambridge, Massachusetts.

"I stole your hat," wrote the author. "I like your hat; I shall keep your hat; whenever I look inside it, I shall think of you and your excellent sherry, and of the town of Cambridge. I take off your hat to you."

# CHAPTER 19

# Don't Change Bosses in Mid-Stream

IT'S NICE to have four years between elections. It takes the voter that long to regain his faith.

Before election the candidate appeals to public opinion. After he's defeated he blames it on herd ignorance and mass stupidity.

The issues in a political campaign are included in the party platform.

What is a party platform? A declaration of unobtainable objectives so phrased as to arouse the maximum confusion with the minimum sincerity.

These declarations of issues are released by politicians with loose memories for consumption by voters who seldom read more than a page of anything unless it has pictures.

For proof of the peculiarity of human nature—this disinclination to overtax our minds—take this incident.

Down in Temple, Texas, some years ago, a reporter on the local paper circulated a petition. The opening paragraph urged President Roosevelt to cut government expenses.

Four hundred residents, including the managing editor of the paper, signed the petition.

The last part of the petition urged the President to appoint Giuseppe Zangara to a cabinet post.

Zangara was the assassin who had attempted to kill the President in Florida some years before.

———•—•———

This might explain the dialogue between father and son while sightseeing in Washington.

"That man, son? He's Chaplain of the Senate."

"Does he pray for the members, dad?"

"No, son. He looks at the members and prays for the country."

———•—•———

Because it was a third party that caused all the trouble in the Garden of Eden, we in the United States have preserved a strict, two-party system.

To preserve America and the two-party institution we check all applicants for government jobs. One chap seeking a janitorial positon was so interrogated.

"Do you belong to any political party advocating the overthrow of the U.S. government?"

"Yes, sir," was the astonishing answer.

"Which one?" asked the interviewer.

"The Republican party," was the answer.

———•—•———

One sweet young thing in the lower ranks of the bureaucratic army was determined not to be caught with her guard down in the government's loyalty probe.

Faithfully filling out the questionnaire intended to expose Communists and fellow travelers on the U.S. payroll, she came to the question demanding a listing of all organizations to which she belonged.

Conscientiously, she wrote: "Van Johnson Fan Club."

———•—•———

Two ward-heelers working for the candidacy of Dowd-for-Alderman were insuring his election by an odd midnight tactic. As revealed in a cartoon by Charles Addams, the two politicians with searchlights are in the cemetery copying down the names of deceased voters.

Another seeker of votes was the orator on the back of the truck. He was in the midst of his spiel when he was heckled. "I'd rather vote for the devil!"

The orator was unruffled. "Suppose your friend does not run? May I count on your support?"

———•———

There was a dinner for the new governor. The grizzled old county chairman, who had never seen the new boss, turned to the lady next to him. "Don't tell me that mugg is the governor?"

"I think you're impudent and crude," she said icily. "Do you know who I am?"

The county leader shook his head.

"I am the governor's wife."

His recovery was instant. "Do you know who I am?"

"No," she said stiffly.

"Good," he replied. "My job is still safe."

———•———

Bob Davis, the diminutive Democratic leader of New Jersey during Woodrow Wilson's era, once attempted to mollify an irate precinct captain.

"Be patient," said Davis, "and soon I'll shake the political plum tree."

"And every time you do," said the other, "nothing but lemons ever drop."

———•———

Dr. Bert Daly, Democratic boss of Bayonne, New Jersey, planned a gigantic rally in the Opera House for Alex Simpson in his campaign for the United States Senate against Dwight Morrow.

There was a huge turnout. The orchestra and first balcony were filled but there was no one in the second balcony. Yet standees and a crowd that overflowed to the sidewalk could have been comfortably seated there.

Daly sent for "Moon" Mahoney, chairman of the Arrangements Committee. "How come there is no one in the second balcony?"

"Boss," answered Moon, "I didn't think you wanted to hire the top floor."

———•———

Bayonne was also the scene of another political meeting where someone's instructions backfired.

The county boss was briefing an Assembly candidate. "When you go down to Bayonne tonight, remember that the most important issue for those people is the large number of trolley poles erected by the traction company. These poles are disfiguring. They lessen property values. And our party is pledged to do something about it."

The candidate spoke fervently that night in Bayonne, but he overlooked one fundamental. Bayonne has a large Polish-American population and this meeting was being held in the Polish Hall.

"You vote for us," shouted the aspirant for the Assembly, "and we'll drive all the poles out of Bayonne."

Then he ducked just in time. The police escorted him out of town.

———•———

They were in one of Boston's periodic political upheavals. And the ubiquitous heckler was challenging the speaker. "What about Curley and his octopuses wrapping themselves about Massachusetts?"

"The plural, Mr. Heckler," said the calm and restrained orator, "is octopi. Remember, you are now in the pie area."

———•———

The quiet retort is always disarming. Mrs. M. V. Hughes in *London at Home* (William Morrow) told of a socialist who once knocked at a house in Park Lane, London, and shouted to the footman: "The Revolution is here!"

"All revolutions must be delivered at the tradesmen's entrance," replied the footman coldly.

———•—•———

One day after Senator Harry S. New had been defeated in a primary contest, he was walking down the stairs in the Capitol to the long tunnel that leads to the Senate Office Building.

A woman visitor to the Capitol, lost and somewhat bewildered by the network of passageways, accosted Senator New. "I am trying to get out of the Senate. Can you tell me how to get out?"

"Madam," said the senator, bowing low, "I advise you to run in an Indiana primary."

———•—•———

Political strategy is always interesting. In the 1932 presidential campaign, Herbert Hoover was endorsed by Mrs. Alton B. Parker, wife of the Democratic presidential candidate of the 1904 campaign.

What the Republican strategists didn't tell the voters was that the lady was Parker's second wife and had always been a Republican.

In the same campaign, the Republican high command also brought elderly Mrs. Theodore Roosevelt out of her Oyster Bay retirement to introduce Herbert Hoover at Madison Square Garden. This was to let the yokels know that the Democratic candidate, Franklin D. Roosevelt, was not Teddy Roosevelt.

You can never be sure that all the voters *will* be aware of the candidate's identity. In a Commission Government election in Irvington, New Jersey, some years ago, the voters elected Harry Stanley commissioner, not knowing that he was the son of a former popular official of the same name.

The father had been dead for several years, but some of the voters didn't know it.

———◆◆———

Margaret Culkin Banning has a favorite political story, too.

When Mrs. Calvin Coolidge went abroad after her husband's death, she feared there would be unnecessary fuss made over the wife of an ex-President. But the friend with whom she was traveling said, "Don't worry. In the little places where we'll be stopping they don't know one president of the United States from another. People won't bother you."

And no one did—until in a small Italian town they received word that reservations for them had been made in the next town. This sounded ominous.

When they reached the hotel in question they were received pompously by the manager. Bowing profoundly, he said, "We are proud to welcome the wife of the great President of the United States. Will you register, Mrs. Lincoln?"

———◆◆———

Ruby A. Meek knew a candidate for county sheriff who was soliciting votes in a small town in Oklahoma. After giving an attentive Negro a fervent campaign speech, he asked for his support.

"Well, Mr. Lee, I tell you, you are my second choice."

The would-be sheriff pondered a moment. Then, concluding that he could easily eliminate the Negro's first choice by maligning the man, he asked cheerfully, "And who's your first choice?"

"Well, sir, just anybody."

———◆◆———

Theodora C. Libbey relates some of the political folklore of New England in this story.

"While on the way to our Vermont village one afternoon,

my mother and I were stopped by a grizzled backwoodsman. " 'Ma'am,' he began uncomfortably, 'just thought I'd
tell you something. Folks say Ben Mitchell's been seen going
to your house more than is fit.'

"Mother's mouth well open. 'Why, Ben Mitchell's an old
married antique with ten children!' she cried indignantly.
'He just comes up to talk to my husband and buy eggs!'

"The farmer scratched his head sadly. 'Ma'am, I see you
don't understand,' he said. 'I guess it's up to me to tell you
folks for your own good. *That man is a Democrat!*' "

A loyal young wife was boasting to a neighbor of the
influence her husband had in politics.

"Yes, indeed," she insisted, "George has voted in two
presidential elections and both times the results have gone
George's way."

A delegation from Kansas, calling upon Theodore Roosevelt at Oyster Bay, was met by the President with coat and
collar off. "Ah, gentlemen," he said, mopping his brow,
"I'm delighted to see you, but I'm very busy putting in my
hay just now. Come down to the barn and we'll talk things
over while I work."

When they reached the barn, there was no hay waiting to
be thrown into the mow. "James!" shouted the President to
his hired man in the loft. "Where's that hay?"

"I'm sorry, sir," admitted James, "but I just ain't had time
to throw it back since you forked it up for yesterday's delegation."

In the House cloakroom where congressmen go to relax
and smoke their tobacco, they're telling the story of two
members who were chatting there.

"My wife told me about the amazing knowledge of parliamentary procedure your wife displayed at the women's club meeting," the first legislator remarked.

"Why not?" shrugged his colleague. "She's been speaker of our house for fifteen years."

---

A political war, according to Phil Kohut, Democratic leader in Long Beach, N. Y., is where everyone shoots from the lip.

---

Before becoming mayor of New York, Bill O'Dwyer ran for district attorney. He generally appeared on the platform with a piece of paper in his hand, ostensibly covered with notes of the address he was about to make.

He'd look around the audience, say "Hello, Joe," to one listener, "Howya, Harry," to another. Then he'd smile and tell the audience: "I didn't know I would have so many friends here tonight. I don't need notes to talk to *you* people," and he'd throw away the paper in his hand. "To you I can speak from here," he'd add, indicating his heart.

A reporter, curious because he had seen O'Dwyer do this in every Brooklyn neighborhood from Red Hook to Brownsville, one night mounted the platform and picked up the discarded paper.

It was an old laundry bill.

---

Abraham Lincoln was an agile-minded courtroom strategist. He was also an able politician. The evidence that a brain was always at work came during his early days in the army.

During the Black Hawk Indian War, Abraham Lincoln was captain of a company, but, unfamiliar with military tactics, he made many blunders. One day when he was marching with a group of over twenty men across a field, he desired to pass through a gate into the next field.

"I could not for the life of me remember the proper command for getting my company endside," said Lincoln

"Finally, as we came near, I shouted: 'This company is dismissed for two minutes, when it will fall in again on the other side of the gate.'"

———•—•———

A strange prophecy came from a philosopher in the bayous when Huey Long was high in power and preaching at all crossroads that he would make "every man a king."

The rough-shaven old fellow listened to these honeyed drippings and said, "He isn't Long for this world."

———•—•———

When Edmund Burke was delivering his famous speech against Warren Hastings, he suddenly stopped in the very middle of an idea. Slowly and impressively he raised his hand and pointed his index finger straight at Mr. Hastings. There he stood for almost a minute with that dramatic pointing finger while the audience almost held its breath. Then he went on.

After the speech one of the opposing advocates came up to him and said, "Mr. Burke, that was one of the most effective pauses I have ever seen. We simply held our breaths, wondering what you were going to say next."

"That," responded Mr. Burke with his Irish twinkle, "is exactly the way I was feeling."

———•—•———

The accent on perpetuation in office is the political knack of being all things to all men. J. R. Lowell explains it in *Biglow Papers*.

> Ez to my princerples, I glory
> In havin' nothin' of the sort.
> I ain't a whig; I ain't a Tory,
> I'm jest a canerdate, in short.

This story is told of Abe Lincoln when he was a candidate for Congress in 1846.

Lincoln attended a preaching service of Peter Cartwright.

Cartwright called on all who wished to go to heaven to stand up. All rose but Lincoln.

Then he asked all to rise who did not want to go to hell. Lincoln still remained seated.

"I am surprised," said Cartwright, "to see Abe Lincoln sitting back there unmoved by these appeals. If Mr. Lincoln does not want to go to heaven and does not want to escape hell, perhaps he will tell us where he does want to go."

Lincoln slowly arose and replied, "I want to go to Congress."

———•—•———

The famous Pepper-Smathers Democratic primary for the U.S. Senate in Florida, 1950, was a torrid campaign.

It may be apocryphal, but Smathers was supposed to have a speech for his illiterate cracker voters that painted his opponent as a man who deserved the gallows. It went this way:

"Are you aware that Claude Pepper is known all over Washington as a shameless extrovert? Not only that, but this man is reliably reported to practice nepotism with his sister-in-law, and he has a sister who was once a thespian in wicked New York. Worst of all, it is an established fact that Mr. Pepper before his marriage habitually practiced celibacy."

———•—•———

Probably the most imperturbable man in the U.S.A. is Dr. George V. O'Hanlon, appointed by former Mayor Frank Hague director of Jersey City's Medical Center.

When Orson Welles made his "scare" broadcast, a student nurse, who had tuned in during the middle of the program and had not heard the explanatory introduction, became hysterical. She ran screaming to Miss Murdoch, Superintendent of Nurses.

"The men from Mars have landed, Miss Murdoch. It's

fearful. They're killing everybody and they're approaching Jersey City." Miss Murdoch switched on her radio and only one minute of the "carnage" was enough for her. She called Dr. O'Hanlon. "The men from Mars landed near Princeton. Some of them reached New York and it is totally destroyed. What shall we do, Doctor? Order out the ambulances, doctors, and nurses? It's fearful. We may all die."

There was a moment's pause and then the dry voice of Dr. O'Hanlon came precisely over the wire. "Let me see. My appointment book is well filled. Tell the men from Mars that I will be able to see them Tuesday morning at eleven."

———•———

Perhaps our over-extended economic lines might eventually have caught up with President Calvin Coolidge. But there are many Americans who'll always associate him with the calm, orderly way of life. And many believe the debacle that caught Herbert Hoover would never have enveloped Cal. The following series of anecdotes give us a real insight into the Coolidge nature.

When Mr. Coolidge was in the Massachusetts legislature, another member in session asked him whether the people where he came from said, "A hen lays, or a hen lies."

"The people where I come from," Mr. Coolidge replied, "lift her up to see."

———•———

The lobby of the hotel was thronged with politicians. The scene was Chicago during the Democratic National Convention.

Up to the desk stepped the old roué. He was well-dressed, well-barbered, and wore a boutonnière that went well with his gold-headed cane.

The girl with him was about twenty-two. She was blonde, buxom, and blank. But she had everything where it ought to be.

The roué registered her. "Your wife?" asked the clerk.

The roué winked and pointed to his delegate's badge. "She's my alternate delegate."

---

A senator of pre-Civil War days, Alexander H. Steven, was less than five feet tall and weighed about ninety pounds.

One day on the Senate floor his mammoth antagonist shrieked at the little fellow, "I could swallow you and never know I ate a thing!"

Little Alex bristled up. "If you did, you'd have more brains in your belly than you have in your head."

---

Frank Allen, who succeeded Coolidge as governor of Massachusetts, visited him in the White House and said: "When I was lieutenant governor under you, I noticed that invariably you finished your work at exactly 5 P.M. Now that I'm governor, I have the same amount of work as you had, but I've never been able to finish it before 9 P.M. Why is it that I can't finish the work by 5 P.M., as you did?"

Coolidge explained: "You talk back."

---

When Calvin Coolidge was President his wife had a portrait painted of him as a surprise. When it was finished, she had it hung in his study. The President was studying it when a senator entered. Coolidge indicated the portrait and the senator gazed at it, too. Neither said a word for fifteen minutes. Then Coolidge said: "I think so, too."

---

Before Coolidge left the White House, his Vermont neighbors decided to recognize his devotion to the old farm by giving him a hand-made rake.

They made the presentation an elaborate ceremonial. The orator who presented the rake dwelt on the qualities of the hickory wood from which, he said, it was made.

"Hickory," he said, "like the President, is sturdy, strong, resilient, unbroken." And so on and on and on. Then he handed the rake to Mr. Coolidge, and the audience settled back for the speech of acknowledgment.

The President turned the implement over, scrutinized it carefully, and then made his address in a single word.

"Ash," he said.

———•—•———

Later, when many people were saying Hoover should be denied a second nomination and that Calvin Coolidge should be drafted, George Horace Lorimer received a telephone call from the former President. Mr. Coolidge wondered if Mr. Lorimer would be interested in buying an article from him stating his attitude toward Mr. Hoover and the Republican Convention. Mr. Lorimer was definitely interested and sent Thomas Costain to Northampton to talk with Mr. Coolidge.

"How much are you prepared to pay me?" asked Mr. Coolidge right off the reel.

"Ten thousand dollars," said Mr. Costain.

Mr. Coolidge studied his shoes for a while, then left the room. Five minutes later he returned. "Ten thousand two hundred and fifty dollars," he said, "and not a penny less." And he walked out again.

Mr. Costain nearly swooned. Had Mr. Coolidge asked for $12,000 or $15,000 but—$10,250 . . . He looked helplessly at Mr. Coolidge's secretary. The latter smiled. "You don't seem to realize," he explained, "that Mr. Coolidge comes from Vermont. He figures that a thing worth $10,000 can be sold for at least two and a half per cent more."

———•—•———

When Harold G. Hoffman was governor of New Jersey, he was asked to visit the inmates of the mental hospital at Greystone Park. The time selected was the Saturday night

party. "It'll be a tonic for them to see you, Governor," said
William J. Ellis, then the top institutional official.

When Governor Hoffman walked into the auditorium, he
noticed that all the inmates were dressed in their Sunday
best. Their hair was combed and their clean, smiling faces
beamed at him. The music was halted.

"Why is it, Commissioner," asked the governor, "that all
the men are on that side of the room and all the women on
the other?"

"Oh," replied Commissioner Ellis, "they're not that
crazy."

Then there was the politician Maurice "Buster" Fleisch-
man knows who paraphrased the automobile slogan:

WHEN BETTER BUCKS ARE MADE
I'LL MAKE 'EM.

# CHAPTER 20

# *Summation*

THE STEREOTYPED GAGS and jokes Dean Ormsby mentions in the earlier pages of this book; the stock, standard cartoons and quips that attack the integrity of the legal profession should be repudiated by the foregoing pages. Yet, just as we close this book, we come upon a poem that begins this way:

> If you've got a son or daughter
> Who ain't livin' like they orter,
> If the neighbors and the preacher,
> The policemen and the teacher
> Are convinced that they are
>     headed straight for hell;
> If their instincts are possessive
> And their ego is excessive,
> If they're short on brains but
>     very long on jaw,
> Don't sit up all night and worry,
> Make your mind up in a hurry,
> Chuck 'em off to school and
>     make 'em study law.

The law colleges today, aware of the disrepute cast on the profession by one dissolute member, are engaged in a highly selective process of choosing young men and women of the best character.

In his advice to the young lawyer, Judge John F. Phillips

of the United States District Court, said: "The profession
you have chosen is among the most exalted that ever engaged the ambition of intellectual men . . . Yours is the
profession to which the present and posterity must look for
the preservation of what is beneficent and cohesive in our
social organism."

———————

There have been giants in the legal profession, men of
great mental attainment who exercised a fine sense of balance and understanding. These are the lawyers who offer
refutation to the critics of the profession. Rufus Choate was
such a giant in his day.

This picturesque leader of the profession had a mackerel-
like complexion and was ill most of his life. His symptoms
were not recognized by medical science at the time but we
would now diagnose them as those of Bright's Disease.

Friends, noting his weakened condition, urged him to rest
that his constitution might be rebuilt.

"My constitution," said Choate, "was destroyed long ago.
I am now living under the by-laws."

———————

Yes, there's more to legal life than chicanery and trickery.
More to it than using the law for unfair advantage. The

JUSTICE

code of ethics governing the profession today could be a guide to all of us. Judge Phillips offers another interesting note of encouragement to the young lawyer. "If you sow and plant and cultivate in dishonor, so will you reap and gather. Common lawyers can be picked up in heaps, for they lie thick about the level waysides; but the excellent ones are at the tops of the rugged steeps."

One who reached the lofty summits was the beloved Oliver Wendell Holmes. Lawyers speak of him as reverently as physicians speak of Hippocrates or Galen. He was a lawyer's lawyer and withal a kindly, humane, considerate person who loved mankind. We like to think of him as the balanced, understanding jurist upon which our foundation of American justice stands. And because this is a book of humor, the following story is recalled.

When Oliver Wendell Holmes was wounded during the Civil War, he was cared for in a Hagerstown, Maryland, home. He lost touch with the family but always remembered their southern charm, particularly that of the daughter. Forty years later he was delighted to receive word that she was coming to Washington and wanted him to dine with her. The understanding Mrs. Holmes laid out her husband's evening clothes and ordered a bouquet for him to take.

At eleven that night she heard the justice come in and go to his study. There was a long silence. Finally she got into a dressing gown, went down and found him at his desk, his head in his hands.

"Wendell," she said softly, "she'd grown fat, hadn't she?"

Only then did he look up. "Yes, my dear," he said meekly.

———•———

When the far distant day dawns when all cases have been discharged by the court, then the lawyer, grown hoary and respected for his role as an advocate of equality and pleader for justice, is now ready to close the books on his own case and to sum up for himself before the greatest tribunal of them all.

Such lines as written by Dorothy Cope Hulse explain this sentimental exit.

> The twilight hour of life has come—
>     A life that was well spent
> A lawyer seeks to lift the load
>     'Neath which his back is bent.
>
> He lifts with care each heavy tome,
>     They stand in neat array;
> He takes them from their dusty home—
>     They're up for sale today.
>
> Each old law book his thin hands stroke,
>     True friends of bygone years.
> A quiv'ring sight for mem'ry's sake
>     Holds back the unshed tears.
>
> He dreams of cases he has had
>     And argued pro and con,
> Of some perchance which he has lost,
>     But most of cases won.
>
> He locks the door, gives up the key,
>     Lifts bravely high his chin,
> With steady tread he starts for home
>     A new life to begin.